The Family Pack

kangaroo dealing with some contact lenses

JOHN HEGLEY

The Family Pack

The Brother-in-Law and Other Animals

Can I Come Down Now Dad?

These Were Your Father's

with drawings by the author

Methuen

With thanks to Andrew, Robert, Nigel, Jackie, Julian and Alison, my regular poetry markers, and to Sue, for decoding my biroed sheaves. And especially to Geoffrey Strachan, editor and initiator of this collection.

11 13 15 17 19 18 16 14 12

This paperback edition published by Methuen 1997

The Family Pack first published in the United Kingdom in 1996 by Methuen, 215 Vauxhall Bridge Road, London SW1V 1EJ

The Brother-in-Law and Other Animals first published in Great Britain in 1986 by the author's own Down the Publishing Company
Can I Come Down Now Dad? first published in Great Britain in 1991 by Methuen London
There Were Your Father's first published in Great Britain in 1994 by Methuen London

Methuen Publishing Limited Reg. No. 3543167

A CIP catalogue record for this book is available from the British Library
ISBN 0 413 71730 5

Typeset by Falcon Oast Graphic art in 11 on 12 point Old Style
Printed and bound in Great Britain by
Cox & Wyman Ltd, Reading, Berkshire

Contents

The Brother-in-Law and Other Animals

Can I Come Down Now Dad?

These Were Your Father's

a fox in the box

a bear in the chair

The Brother-in-Law
and Other Animals

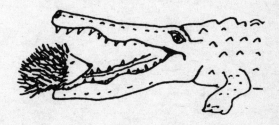

a pain in the neck

His heart's in the wrong place — it should be in the glove compartment

after his favourite vegetarian meal
consisting of seventeen pints of lager
my brother-in-law offers me a lift home
on the way we stop off for a drink
at the bar I ask for two halves of lager
my brother-in-law says there is no such thing as a
   half of lager
I suggest we get the bus the rest of the way
my brother-in-law says that buses are only for
   scum
and that if he comes in his car
he leaves his car
before we leave and discover that his car has been
   stolen
my brother-in-law tells me
how he likes to stop and ask hitch-hikers where
   they are going
and then tells them that he will get there first

I wouldn't say my brother-in-law was fat because he is quite thin

he's as miserable as sin
but not as interesting
he's as open as the pub is at twenty past four
in the morning
and as welcome as an open sore
on your eye
but he thinks he is great
he isn't beautiful
he's horrible
he eats crisps in the cinema as a matter of
    principle
in a previous incarnation he was a beer crate
if he does you a favour then you know that
    you're in debt
if you want someone to help you he's a very
    outside bet
if you were in a lifeboat and someone had to go
and my brother-in-law was there
you wouldn't exactly need a ballot
he's ten stone in his pyjamas
and that's ten stone overweight
he's not exactly an artist
but they should hang him in the Tate
he was an adult from the age of eight
and whatever age he dies at will be far too late
I don't like him

The brother-in-law's dream

in his dream his hair turns into snakes
in his sleep he rips out his hair
in the morning
he wakes up and says
it's a good job it was only a dream
unaware that in the night
he has completely balded himself

His heart's in the wrong place — it should be in the dustbin

the other night I went to see my brother-in-law
   for a chat
after five minutes he went and sat in the garage
after ten minutes he came back in saying
here John are you staying the night?
if that's all right I said
then he was gone
up to the spare bedroom
to change the sheets
to put the dirty ones back on

___ Counterfeit love _____

down in the cellar
there's a feller
he is bald and he's called Peter
he's got a lot of money but that's not so funny
on account of the boy's a counterfeiter
he moistens a thumb and he flicks through a
    grand
his chum does the same and he pockets a pony
his nickname is Nick
and his real name is Tony
meanwhile upstairs there's another note
that has just been wrote in biro
it says dear Tony I have only just discovered
that your love is phoney too
and I'm leaving
you
you could say I'll be forging my own way
but you probably won't

The firework

up in the sky go the rockets
little Albert gets a big surprise
and his big round eyes
light up in their sockets
the rockets
came out of his trouser pockets

The firework two

he held the burning roman candle
an outdoor firework without a handle
it made him cough
some bits flew off
and turned his shoe into a sandal

Christmas

there came three wise men from the East
and so it came to pass
the wise men found the shepherds
a bit working class

Christmas with the brother-in-law (oh what fun)

the two clip-on earrings slip from our Christmas
    cracker
you can have them John
my brother-in-law quips
I slip into the earrings
how do I look then handsome?
I lie to him
all right John very sexy take them off
he says trying to sound normal in his torn
    Christmas hat
that is sat around his neck
you're not a woman
he reminds me
how do you explain these then?
I reply ripping open my shirt and squirting my
    nipples at him
shall I take these off too?
don't spoil the Christmas John
my mother interrupts

Sister

sister you are an alchemist
base metals into gold you cannot do
but I have seen you
turn boredom into joy
and make toys from the rubbish
sister you are an alchemist
but you have not done a very good job
with your husband

Edinburgh

I'm afraid I won't be going to the Edinburgh
    tattoo
because to me
a parade of weaponry
and the capacity to hurt
is about as pleasing as dog dirt
on the shoe
only poo
is easier than the tattoo
to get rid of

to you
it may be taboo
to poo-poo
the tattoo
but to me
the tattoo
is something to say ta-ta to

Glasgow

as we walk across the bridge across the Clyde
I talk of the tide
and the spring
and the spring in the suspension
but do not mention our tension
is there any hope of a bridge over that divide
Stephen
a rope even
or must we remain as strangers
like the Pope and Glasgow Rangers

Amsterdam

in Amsterdam
I saw a tram

The imagination

the only nation worth defending
a nation without alienation
a nation whose flag is invisible
and whose borders are forever beyond the
    horizon
a nation whose motto is why have one or the
    other
when you can have one the other and both
a nation whose badge is a chrysanthemum of
    sweet wrappings
maybe
a nation whose laws are magnificent
whose customs are not barriers
whose uniform is multiform
whose anthem is improvised
whose hour is imminent
and whose leader is me

I need you

I need you like a bully needs to boast
I need you like an ocean needs coast
I need you like a dog needs a lamppost

I want you

I want you like my crumpled trousers want a
    press
I want you like Rumpelstiltskin
wanted the princess
to guess
I want you like a naked somnambulist
out walking on a cold winter's night
on waking wants to dress

Choking each other off

we know each other in the cyclical sense
we make each other sick
we are each other's oil slick
we are each other's poorly maintained public
  convenience
there is too much we
I am yours and you are mine
and yet it started out so well
so fine
so bright
such joy
our relationship is a firework
that fell into the toilet

Amoeba

hello amoeba I wish you were my pet
but you're not really big enough to be seen by
   the vet
are you?
you're a little blob of jelly
you've got no skin and bone
you're not a boy you're not a girl
and you're not on the telephone
I cannot get in touch with you
I cannot pull your leg
you look a bit like a fried egg
you're a long way down the ladder
that evolution trod
but you can eat with your feet
or to be more discreet
obtain food with your pseudopod
and you don't have to have a partner
to start a family
you can multiply by dividing
tra-la-la-la-lee
you don't get up in the morning
because you never go to bed
you've not got any genitalia
but you've got other bits instead
I saw you down the microscope
when I was just a lad
I told my mum about you
and then I told my dog
you're not heterosexual bisexual

transvestite transsexual
lesbian or gay
but you seem to do okay
it isn't rude to be an amoeba
in the nude
is it eh?
you're not so simple
you little protoplasmic pimple

Private

there's a notice in my drive it says private
that's the way to stay alive
in private
don't look into my windows
don't look into my eyes
I'm not a public enterprise
I don't hold hands or give my heart
I am one big private
part
personal questions waste my time
it's none of your business
if it's any of mine
don't ask me if I've got the time
don't ask me if I've got a light
I might have
but then again I might not
what's it got to do with you?
nothing
I sometimes cry a tear or two
but I find a toilet before I do
it's the kind of thing I always do
in private
I don't know why I'm telling you

In class

by chance I glance at her answer paper
protective of her labour
my next-door neighbour
drops an accusing karate chop
across the page-top
to stop me from copying
as she writes
her name

Liverpool

on the ferry across the Mersey
it was cold
and I wore my jersey

Glastonbury

it is the peace festival
midnight
moonlight
and the sound of drumbeat and song
as long as the night is
a night of dancing chanting rhythm and release
it is the festival of peace
and there's nowhere round here you can get any

Amen

surely it should be A man
or some men
and if it's some men
how many?
is it just the big two
the father and son
or is it one or two men more
or is it many more men
or is it all men
or is it just no women?
(eh men?)

In the cell

in the cell
there are spelling mistakes everywhere

Seaing the sea

knee deep in the ocean
something in the ever-steady knee-cap lapping
   motion
of the ocean
moves me to emotion
something infinitely playful
something totally and finally benign
in the briny
makes these four eyes of mine wet with weep
(as if there wasn't enough salt water already)

In a boat in Plymouth harbour

about to embark
on a tour of the bay
we pay our one-pound-fifties
and we're off
good morning ladies and gentlemen
here we are at the mouth of the Tamar
to your right is Devon and on your left is
    Cornwall
now that's interesting
I'd forgotten how the river forms a natural
    boundary
between the two counties
I remember old Taffy Bennett telling us that in
    geography
well that's twenty-five-pence worth already
and on your right again is a statue of King
    William of Orange
mmm – just how I'd imagined him
only bigger
and up ahead there you can see a nuclear
    submarine
oh dear
I do hope we don't have a war
I wave to a man working on the deck of the sub
but he does not wave back
it is my brother-in-law

Armadillo

my mummy she bought me an armadillo
I kissed him and kept him under my pillow
and I cleaned him with a Brillo pad
he was shiny and tiny he came from Peru
his name was Armadeus
but we used to call him Toby
he had a suit of armour and he burrowed about
the hills and the daffodils he turned them inside
out
and my mother used to shout at him
when he came home covered in graffiti
he was an insectivorous creature
the teacher used to say
and the dog next door
the carnivore
would sometimes come and play
we had races and chases down by the riverside
and sometimes we'd go swimming and
sometimes we wouldn't
he had ants and beetles for dinner every day
them creepy-crawlies he could put 'em away
and he did his indoor doings
in his indoor doings tray
but one day in the winter
when the willow was bare
I looked under my pillow
and there was nobody there
I ran downstairs and I said to my mummy
mummy where's he gone?

she was having a game of rummy
and she looked up and she said John
go and put some clothing on
you're nearly twenty-four
and I said sorry Mum it's an emergency
and I ran out in the raw
I ran down to the riverside
and in a rowing boat I saw
Armadeus
in the distance
with the dog next door

INSECTS

Jimmy Greaves

it's not much of a planet
that everybody leaves
there's not a lot of faith about
but I am someone who believes
that what we need without a doubt
is more of Jimmy Greaves
imagine Jimmy's picture in every picture frame
imagine all religion praising Jimmy's name
the world is just a candle
and Jimmy Greaves is the flame
won't you gimme Jimmy
the more I get of Greavsie
the more my life achieves
so give me more of Greavsie
and more of Jimmy Greaves
it used to be his turn of speed.
he left defences in a daze
now he rents his turn of phrase
and when I turn on my TV
and Jimmy's there
my spirits raise
and when I'm in a blazing row
and I'm in the process of rolling up my sleeves
I just think of Greavsie
and he relieves me
more and more of Greavsie
is what this country needs
he's the man to sow the seeds of sanity
he's off the booze he's on the ball

he's got a message for us all
he can help humanity
to heal itself
to haul itself
from this self-destructive stupor
he's what you call a trooper
I think he's blinking super
he's a trooper super duper
so please don't give me Henry Cooper
he isn't Jimmy Greaves
people say that I'm loopy
they think I'm nothing
but a Greavsie groupie
but I tell them
you're not fit to wash
Jimmy Greaves's moustache

The man in the street

the other day I met a bloke
lying on the pavement
he'd just had a stroke
and I thought a man in his position
might appreciate a joke
so I said stand back please I'm a comedian

The children in the park

in the park
the children are playing a game of kiss chase
and one of the children
who seems to want to be chased after
calls out above the screams and laughter
don't chase me!
don't chase me!
and nobody does

A dog and a pigeon

in a shocking flurry of feathers
a seemingly pleasant dog attacked a pigeon in
    the park
the badly shaken owner tethered the attacker
who began to bark
if that dog can kill I said
you should let it finish the job
no said another witness
it's not our job to interfere with nature
the owner looked
the pigeon bled
it's your dog – your decision I said
I'll let him go, says the owner
and then it's up to Fred
so Fred is freed
and the bleeding bird
is shaken and left but still not dead
it's even worse now the owner whimpers
a brick on the head then I say
I can't says the owner beginning to weep
can you – can you do it?
then my brother-in-law comes over
with half a paving stone
I'll do it he says
for ten quid

The deep-end

you deep end on me

Can I Come Down
Now Dad?

Luton

*(a poem about the town of my upbringing and the
conflict between my working-class origins and the
middle-class status conferred upon me by a university
education)*

I remember Luton
as I'm swallowing my crout'n

___ When the Queen came to Luton ___

I felt awkward
seeing my mother openly overjoyed and childlike
shaking her flag
and making a din
and advising me to do the same
if I didn't want a good hiding
when my father came in

___ Super sunburn ___

super sunburn
is what my brother
called the bright right handprints
that my Dad would add to my arms and legs
when I was bad
he thought up the title
one night while he was eating my supper
regular burns were handed out
for shouting at my sister
when she failed to collect the rent
after I had landed on one of her properties in
    Monopoly
but the biggest attack
was for when my Dad said he was fed up
to the back teeth with me
and I pointed out that he never had any back teeth
my brother said that the marks I received on this
    occasion
were excellent

My Dad's new belt

when my Dad bought his new belt
the woman who sold it to him
told him that it was very strong
and would probably last longer than he would
and my Dad said that he would give it to one of
   his children

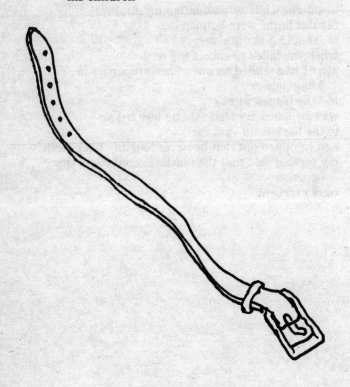

Eddie don't like furniture

Eddie don't go for sofas or settees
or those little tables that you have to buy in threes
the closest thing that Eddie's got to an article of
    furniture's
the cheese board
Eddie doesn't bolster the upholstery biz
there's a lot of furniture in the world but none of it's
    Eddie's
he won't have it in the house however well it's made
Eddie's bedroom was fully furnished
when the floorboards had been laid
and Eddie played guitar
until he decided that his guitar was far too like
an article of furniture
Eddie offers visitors a corner of the room
you get used to the distances between you pretty soon
but with everyone in corners though
it isn't very easy when you're trying to play pontoon
    or happy families
he once got in a rowing boat and they offered him a
    seat
it was just a strip of timber but it wasn't up his street
he stood himself up in the boat and made himself feel
    steady
then he threw the plank onto the bank and said
furniture?
no thank you
when it's on a bonfire furniture's fine
any time that Eddie gets a number twenty-nine bus

even if there's seats on top and plenty down below
Eddie always goes where the pushchairs go
does Eddie like furniture?
I don't think so
if you go round Eddie's place and have a game of hide
and seek
it isn't very long before you're found
and in a fit of craziness Eddie took the legs off his dash
hound
that stopped him dashing around
Eddie quite likes cutlery
but he don't like furniture
if you give him some for Christmas
he'll returniture

My doggie don't wear glasses

my doggie don't wear glasses
so they're lying when they say
a dog looks like its owner
aren't they

Memory

my sister loved animals
she was always taking the dog out
and stroking it
and the goldfish

Reflection

my Mum used to spend so long cleaning the
    mirror
you could see her face in it
(if you used your imagination)

John was feeling a bit lonely
so he decided to pretend that his portable telly was a
    little dog
the screen was its face
the cable was its tail
the aerial was its ear
and the screws at the back
they were its little fleas
John was very happy with his new friend
until one day she became very ill
after John had given her a bath
when the repair man came
John called out IT'S ALL RIGHT PET
THE VET'S HERE!
and the repair man asked John if he was sick
and John explained that it was not him that was sick
it was his little dog
and he led the man into the living room
and showed him his portable telly all wrapped up in
    blankets
and the repair man took out a big screwdriver
and pushed it into John's throat
oh great said John
you're going to get rid of her little fleas as well are you?
but the repair man thought he was teasing
and he took hold of John and he hit him
and the portable telly jumped up and bit him

Pat

I said Pat
you are fat
and you are cataclysmically desirable
and to think I used to think
that slim was where it's at
well not any more Pat
you've changed that
you love yourself
you flatter yourself
you shatter their narrow image of the erotic
and Pat said
what do you mean FAT?

___ On the ward ___

once when I worked in a hospital
one boy chewed the wheels
of another boy's wheelchair so badly
that it rolled along very lumpily
and had to be sent to the menders

Colin

Colin was a vandal and when certain things were said
he flew off the handle and he banged you in the head
he went down the hospital to get it sorted out
the doctor said good morning and Colin knocked him
   out
Colin said I'm sorry doctor can you make me sane
the doctor said we'll sort you out and took out Colin's
   brain
cell
when Colin left the hospital he was miserable
what was he to do instead of banging people in the
   head?
but then one day he walked into a lamppost in the
   street
and discovered self expression aggravating concrete
soon he was as right as rain
and he couldn't complain at all
he got himself a little job as a demolition ball
now Colin does a hard day's work
comes home at half past five
calls out Mum it's me I'm home and I'm still alive
then he runs into the living room
gets stuck into the wall
and his Mum says show some consideration Colin
do it in the hall
and by the way your dinner's in the safe

John Hegarty's cap

one day I came home from school
and my Mum said that cap's not yours
and sure enough it was not
it was John Hegarty's
a boy with a name like mine
and a cap like mine
you don't know where it's been she said
throwing it onto the fire

These National Health glasses

these National Health glasses were devised
before the vision of the people got privatised

In the arms of my glasses

they can call me softy
as ofty
as they please
but still I'll stand by these
my little optical accessories
they stop me walking into lampposts
and trees
when it's foggy
and I'm out walking with my doggie

The briefcase

from the very beginning I loved my glasses
the eye test made me feel important
I wanted to be colour blind as well
for some reason
I was never teased about them as a child
not even at the grammar school
where daily they would mock my briefcase
because it was not made of leather
as I recall there was only ever one boyhood jibe
aimed at my glasses
and this a fairly oblique one
OI DOUBLE GLAZING
WHERE DID YOU GET THAT PLASTIC
    BRIEFCASE?
in adult years I got a lot more trouble
on one occasion
a rabble
threw rubble
at my glasses
it was after this that I decided to take action
I bought myself a leather briefcase
and the next day set out to face my building site
    tormentors
somehow the briefcase in my hand
was a stand
against a land

which had gradually lost its magic for me
a joyful absurdity
in the face
of the tragically commonplace
as I approached the contractors
for once it felt like MY world again
what have you got in the briefcase then four eyes?
was the question
POWER was the reply
the power of the human imagination
and I walked proudly
and steadily past them
in a shower of flying masonry

Go and play in the middle

my Mum used to watch out of the window
these boys who played football
on the green in front of our bungalow
she used to stand well back
so she couldn't be seen
and when the ball hit the wall of our garden
she said to my Dad
it's hit our wall again Bob
go out and tell them
and my Dad would go out and tell them
maybe eight or nine times in a day
to go and play in the middle
and immediately he had told them
my Mum would be on the watch
for the next time he would need sending out
and sometimes it was only a few moments
after he had come back in

A comparison of logs and dogs

both are very popular at Christmas
but it is not generally considered cruel
to abandon a log
and dogs are rarely used as fuel

Loggie

____ In the name of the Lord _____

J   just like his Dad

E   ever so just (like his Dad)

S   speckless (he never wore glasses)

U   unable to swim   ●

S   sometimes I wonder if he was praying for
the betraying kiss of Judas so as not to miss out
on his Easter egg

C   cut bread into very thin slices

H   hippy aeroplane impressionist

R   really easy to spot in a crowd on a Good Friday

I   I wonder if he had a dog

S   escapologist

T   took him three days but he did it

The hearing difficulty

when she was about nine
unbeknown to the rest of the family
my sister filled in a newspaper coupon
requesting further information
from a hearing aid company in London
and a representative travelled the thirty-two miles
to our home in Luton
to give more information about the product
realising that it was not enough to say 'not today thank
   you'
or 'we're not interested in God'
my mother burst into the living room
where Angela and I were playing Monopoly
and demanded an explanation for the preposterous
   arrival
Angela said there was a girl in her class
who was a bit deaf
and she thought a little hearing aid would be of help
my mother then dragged her out to the front door
to repeat the story
so the man could see that he was dealing with an idiot

On the booze

My dad very rarely drank
but one time when he did
my mother blew her lid rather
and leaving the lather
and the sink
she said you stink
you stink of drink
you've tried to hide it with a peppermint
but I don't think it's done the job
because you blinking stink Bob
it's obnoxious
let some air through
open the windows will you
and the door.
He had had two halves of lager
Three days before.

___ He saw his dinner on TV ___

one day John cooked up his favourite
sausage chips and curried beans
and hurried into the living room
eager to consume the nourishment
he sat himself down in front of the telly
and his mouth fell open wide
there wasn't any food on his fork though
it was something on the screen
he was tellyfied
he'd never seen anything like it
well he had – that was the trouble
the sausage was the same sausage
the beans were the same beans
even the chips in the chips were the same
the plate was different – the cutlery was utterly
   different
but the dinner was exactly the same
the only occasion on which John had experienced
anything out of the ordinary before
was an occasion on which a letter came
through the door
that was actually meant for his next-door neighbour
but nothing like this
there was a knock at the door
it was John's new neighbour
she handed him a postcard
depicting detail for detail
the very bowl of jelly he had prepared for his afters
then John's dog walked in

a dog which incidentally he had buried the previous
    evening
that night John couldn't sleep
so he got up
and emptied a few marshmallows into a shallow dish
as a little treat for himself
there were seven of them – six white and one pink
and they looked so appetising
that John took a polaroid snapshot of them
as a kind of memento
he then plucked the pink marshmallow
sucked it
swallowed it
and turned to the photo to remind himself of his
    favourite
but there was no pink marshmallow in the photo

___ Steamed pudding ___

at our school you had to have everything
and you had to eat everything
and for some years
I would slip my steamed pudding in my pocket
disposing of it later in the playground bin
but one day I decided I was too old to behave like this
and I put my hand up and said please Miss
I can't eat this steamed pudding
and Miss said that I was mistaken
and I would have all lunch break
and after school if necessary
and possibly the rest of my life to prove it
she got back to her task of crossing out people's work
and left me with mine
it was slow – unpleasant
three quarters of an hour of held breath
and pretending to be anywhere but the present
but eventually there was no more steamed pudding to
    be seen
my bowl scraped as clean as someone who loved the
    stuff
neatly and quietly I put down my spoon
then she put down her pen
and smiled
not the smile she had when she was caning someone
but the smile of someone who has asked you
to demonstrate your love by doing the impossible
and unaccountably
it has been done

a smile as if she understood
how I hated steamed pud
I want to give you something for doing that she said
those mouthfuls weren't enough to feed a little mouse!
and I imagined an outrageous benevolence
possibly the confiscations of another boy
possibly a million points for my house
probably a joy beyond my imagining
she beckoned me close
and from out of her desk
she handed me a second helping

Bad news

when I used to write my daily news
I nearly always went over the page
and the boy sitting next to me never
for him three lines was a good endeavour
but one day he wrote three and a half pages
and he said to me SEE
you're not the only one who's clever
and he went and showed it to Miss
and Miss showed it to the class
look at all these words she said
they make no sense whatsoever

One day while we were getting out our rough books

one day while we were getting out our rough
    books
there was a bit of chattering
and Miss went all red and said stop stop stop
STOP STOP STOP
and we were very quiet
and Miss went more red and said
there is something the matter with the children
in class Two Purple
do you know what you are?
DO YOU KNOW WHAT YOU ARE?
and we were very very frightened
and we did not know what we were

The martian

there was a young creature from space
who entered a three-legged race
he was not very fast
in fact he came last
because he was a bag of oven-ready chips

The play

yesterday I went to see a play in my friend's car
it was by an experimental group
who do plays in people's cars

The snub

at school I used to play a lot of 'Subbuteo'
(a table football game)
and they used to call me Sub
and it was good to have a nickname
until they told me it stood for sub-human

The scouting outing

there was Green Green
who fell in the latrine
and when Redman said to Green
let's go and dig a latrine
he didn't mean with shovels
he meant let's form a latrine appreciation society
and there was Joe
who brought his blow-football along
and there was Strong
who beat him every game
and there was one lad
who had never seen blow-football before
whose name I can't remember
and there was Tony Ward
whose folks couldn't afford a uniform
but he'd just got himself a paper-round
and anyway the campfire's warm
welcomed every colour creed and parental income
   bracket
and there was Skip Skip
with his artificial hip
and there was Joe
saying I don't know if I want to go
pulling out people's tent pegs
and there was Redman calling him a drip
and there was Dorking talking about sleeping
and keeping the peace by saying Joe
was nowhere near as big a drip as Green
(whose Dad was in the police)
there was a village shop to pillage

tuck under torchlight
and the never-ceasing porchlight of the tall frame tent
which meant our leader needn't crouch and crawl
and he could keep an eye out
through the little plastic windows in the wall
oh the joy of it all
on that boy scout jamboree
never having heard of the likes of CND
never doubting there'd be scouting for our children
with the jumbo campfire kettle
forever spouting tea
if they'd had a badge for being optimistic
I imagine they'd have given one to me

Skip

___ Dad's dark glasses _____

sometimes when my Dad was watching the telly
he would fell asleep
and my Mum would shake him and say
go to bed Bob will you if you're knackered
and he would wake up and try to look alert
but one day he said the glare from the telly was hurting
    his eyes
and he would need some dark glasses
and from that day on
you couldn't tell if he was asleep
or watching the telly

The wizard that was

his pointed hat is pointless
his magic wand's a stick
his dog could do better tricks with
if she hadn't run away
he can say every word the spell book says to say
and wave his arms about all day
but he's powerless
he couldn't cast a shepherd
in a school nativity play

The genie in the wireless

one day John turned on his radio
and heard a voice say hello I'm the genie in your
    wireless
if you're a genie why aren't you in a bottle?
John snapped at what he thought was another stupid
    advert
and slightly hurt the genie replied
you could say I've lost my bottle couldn't you John?
but only because you always tend to state the obvious
realising that the genie was probably real
John immediately demanded his three wishes
so you only want me for what you can get then?
enquired the lonely force
of course replied John indignantly
why else does anybody want anyone?
for what they can give?
suggested the genie
OK John replied so give me a great big car!
how beautifully humble remarked the machine's
    unseen ghost
how wholly imaginative
not like the last person who asked me for a piece of
    peanut brittle
and wanted to be the rainbow in the bubble
of a trouble-maker's spittle
that's right agreed the other slightly confused
nothing like it – I want a big car
and I want to be able to drive
all right but that's your lot said the voice in the radio

no it's not that's only one wish
two at the most John complained
and the genie explained about the cuts
in the magical services industry
and told him that there was a march if he was
    interested
the only March I'm interested in
is the one that comes after April
said John making a bit of a mistake

__ Mr McNaulty __

one day Mr McNaulty left the launderette to get some
  fags
and these boys came in with laundry bags
and unloaded a number of small dogs
into one of the tumble driers
as they fumbled with the faulty coin mechanism
Mr McNaulty returned
OH NO YOU DON'T he cried
pushing them aside
and pulling out the dogs
these driers are for washing machine customers only

Skip

Train spotters

OK so some of us wear anoraks
and some of them have hoods with fur on
and some of us drink quite a bit of cocoa
but it doesn't mean we're loco

everybody's looking out for something
that may be round the bend
we just tend to do it with a duffle bag
but we're train spotters
we're not trend setters
and a platform ticket takes us
just as far as we want to go
– to the end of the platform show

is taking down another person's underwear
being any more alive
than taking down a one-two-five's little details?
OK so we may be wetter
but it is better than drying
the wet that you get from crying
over a love that is dying

is the happy shunter hunter
any more insane
than the lot who've not got jotters
who spot the spotty spotters
with disdain?
we're looking forward to our crusty rolls
we've got platform tickets

and platform souls
it's a passion
not a fashion show
it's smashen' though

___ Well bred dog ___

one evening John came home from work
went into the kitchen to make himself a nice cup of tea
and on the kitchen table in a plastic bag
he discovered a large sliced loaf with one of the crusts
    missing
actually it was a VERY large sliced loaf
about the size of a rabbit hutch
and John who lived very much alone
knew that he hadn't put it there and wondered who
    had
just then there was a rap a tat tat at the front door
it was John's new next-door neighbour
excuse me barging in she said
but you haven't seen my dog have you?
what does it look like enquired John concernèdly
like a large sliced loaf replied the neighbour
with one of the crusts missing asked John
yes replied the neighbour she had a fight
John smiled
went out into the kitchen
and returned with the mysterious loaf
is this her by any chance he asked
and the neighbour said no

___ Well executed poem ___

before the blast of the squad
his last request
was a bullet-proof vest
or a God

I am going

there is not a rumour
of humour
in the tumour
of our life
I am going
I am stifled
I am going
I am going
to survive
you would do anything for me
except go
it is me not you
who makes you feel alive
I am going
I'll be back about five

__ On the bus _____

for a while I was a bus conductor
and one day my Dad got on my bus
and sat on the long seat next to my cubby hole
he was proud to see me in a uniform and a job
and in a loud voice he said to everyone
do you remember the bus conductor's outfit you had
when you were a boy John?
and I said no Dad
but I remember how you used to enjoy beating me

Poetry

poetry don't have to be
living in a library
there's poetry that you can see
in the life of everybody,
a lick of paint's the kind of thing I mean
a lick of paint's a lovely piece of writing
the tongue of the paintbrush
giving something drab
a dab new sheen
a lick of paint's exciting.

there are folk who like to see
Latin in their poetry
and plenty of obscurity
me for instance
(only joking)
how I like to listen to the lingo
in bingo
legs eleven
clickety-click
a lick of paint
no – sorry that ain't one

poetry – language on a spree
I want to be
a leaf on the poetree
poetry is good for me
I think I'll have some for my tea

String

If you're depressed
and your life don't mean a thing
pop into a hardware shop
and cop hold of some string

My old cap

Before I get sat in the café
I take my flat cap off my hair
and place it in the lap
of the uncharitable chair.
It makes a good little cushion
but unfortunately I leave it there.
I do not realise that this is where
I have left it, until a week's time
when I'm in the café once more
and my order is taken by a chap
who is jauntily wearing my cap.

Going to Virgin Records

On the underground
a man communicates in sign language
and I listen to the sound of his
anorak.

___ A spectacular tale _____

Once I had a whitehead on the bridge of my nose in the
shape of a railway engine which made the wearing of
my glasses uncomfortable, but being shortsighted, and
because I was only doing close-up work at the time,
I felt able to remove my old friends, placing them
carefully into the home of their case, which in turn
I positioned in the inside pocket of my shirt. During
the next half an hour or so I ventured into no form of
human bustle where someone might have interfered
with the case and if an intruder had tried to sneak into
the room taking advantage of my poor eyesight, my
keen-eyed dog John would certainly have noticed and
sounded the alarm. However when I did finally go
out and I removed the case myself I discovered a pair
of spectacles identical to the ones I had recently
removed.

Only they were made entirely of plasticine!

A little story which I have given certain
embellishment: the spot was not railway-engine
shaped, the inside pocket of my shirt was of course a
jacket pocket and, most significantly, I omitted to
relate that on positioning the plasticine spectacles on
my face, I experienced a terrible sense of my own
mortality as it struck me that during my life I would
only remove and replace my glasses a specific number
of times. The thought filled me with sombreness to the
extent that I began to weep, removing the glasses so
that I could wipe my eyes, thus adding one more to
whatever the final number would otherwise have been;

the realisation of which cheered me to such an extent
that I decided to take John for an additional walk
around the house.

_____ A walk around the house _____

you've been both a good dog and a bad dog
and I have got some good news and some bad
the good news is we're going for a walkies
but it won't be the longest walkies you have ever had

off we go then
here's the hall
no – we're not going out at all
there's the stairs
that's the way
let's be different
today

up we go then
not so fast
if you want this walk to last you
here's my bedroom
there's my pit
where's the walkies?
this is it

have a sit down
rest your paws
there's a bit of a mess
now – can you guess which bit of it is yours?

Smothering Sunday

To a wonderful mother
with wrinkly skin,
this card was concocted
by one of your kin.
I hope that you like it
it's specially for you,
I've sprinkled some glitter
on top of some glue.
I don't like the bought ones
I thought you should know,
they're too superficial
and two quid a throw
some of them.

The Easter Story
according to St Bernard

When they came to take his boss away
the apostle with the sword
smote the servant's ear off
and got told off by the Lord,
who replaced the lackey's lug'ole
saying not to be so rude,
but not before a naughty dog
had thought someone had given her
a little scrap of food.
And that undignifying Friday
when it seemed they'd sealed His doom
the dog that chewed the ear up
got to end up in the tomb,
and by the Sunday morning
she was dying to be fed
and she barked and she barked loud enough
to waken up the dead,
which she did.

On Hampstead Heath

I ask you what sort of tree
we are sat underneath
and you tell me that it is a big one.
You ask me how I came by the scar on my knee
and I tell you that I hurt myself once.
A passer-by, possibly Austrian
and possibly a Christian,
points to a fluorescent cycle clip in the grass
and wonders if I might have lost it.
I stand up and indicate that I am wearing shorts.

What we have been

We have been too eager
to learn each other's secrets
and now we're not so keen
we are like the wings of a moth
without the moth bit in between.

The photos of the divorce

The ones at the end
(after the flying saucers)
the ones of them coming apart,
they came out so much better
than the wedding pictures,
there was no confetti in the camera
for a start.

Making confetti

The North Yorkshire Moors Railway
is a coal-burning journey
fuelled by love and enthusiasm.
I collect my thick oblong of ticket
at the start
and an inspector's hole
in the shape of a heart
somewhere in the middle.

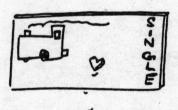

Train window pain

gazing through the glazing
glasses pressed on glass
sad eyes on the shining track
going back
to town

Off the rails

the ticket inspector said I'm a defector
but spoke like a native and broke into song
he sang about cricket whilst building a wicket
and Stephenson's 'Rocket' came rolling along

and out of the Rocket stepped old Davey Crockett
who waved to his mother and went in to bat
I'm cracking at cricket and I've got no ticket
he said showing off in his usual hat.

The backwoodsman's Mum said I'm coming old chum
and she bowled an alarm clock from out of the blue
and the man at the sticks said I'll knock it for six
even though it's been set for a quarter to two

Crockett was out he was too busy talking
and as he was moodily walking away
the East German sector born ticket inspector
said if you've no ticket there's money to pay

the disgruntled Crockett dipped into his pocket
and in the confusion he ended his life
he threw down his hat and let go of his bat
and then slowly keeled over on top of his knife

the sky went all cloudy
his last word was howdy
his mother then said of the deed
oh what a business
my boy's lost his is-ness
the ticket inspector agreed

Camping for pleasure

After I'd gone on my first bit of camping with the
    scouts
I went to the public library and got a book out
called Camping For Pleasure
in which there was a bit about how to make
a trip to the toilet more comfortable
by taking a saw to the seat
of a worn-out wooden chair
and taking out a circle of the appropriate size.
After I had attempted to realise this contraption
my mother seriously contested my concept of worn-out
with reference to the kitchen chair of my choosing
that she was losing
and my father demonstrated that if nothing else
there was still plenty of wear left in the discarded seat
for beating purposes.

In Edinburgh

I'm in the Botanic Gardens gallery,
a man pushes past me
to look at a beautiful picture
without saying pardon.
I want to point a sizzling finger
and make his arteries harden
to the stiffness of the depicted stone,
a feeling Festival artists are known
to have directed at the Press
which has been putting a picture
alongside the stinkingest review
to make the unwitting performer think
'oh look it's me'
and then be
particularly unpleasantly surprised
by the accompanying poison.

Christmas in the doghouse

It was Christmas day in the doghouse,
and no one had a bone,
and one dog who was desperate
was chewing up the phone-book,
when suddenly to their surprise
a canine Santa came
and luckily they had no logs
or he'd have been aflame.

Good news I bring the Santa said
('cos he knew how to speak)
from now on I'll be visiting the doghouse
once a week,
we'll break the human habit
they seem to hold so dear;
good will to fellow creatures,
but only once a year.
It's true we tend to urinate
around the Christmas tree,
but we're fit to lead
and not be led
in spreading Christmas glee.

They didn't want a sermon though
that's not why he was there
they all piled in like vermin
to his sack of Christmas fare,
and they eated all the bones up
and they treated Santa rough,
and as he left the doghouse
he said once a year's enough.

God plays I spy

I spy with my little eye
something beginning
with sinning
that's not as nice as paradise
and I have to send my son down twice
to save it

The miracle and the people

the statue on the pilgrimage
is bleeding from the hands
and asking for a handkerchief
but no one understands
Latin any more

The Romans

they had planning restrictions
they had tenement flats with balconies
and café meeting places on the ground floor
they had central heating
central government
and fire brigades
they even had those little things
you put under indoor flower pots
to stop any spillage
when the plants have been watered

Watling Street

Just off the Old Kent Road
I dig them digging
in the archaeological way
the Roman way to Chester,
these are shards of flagon
possibly flung from a passing wagon
I'm told.
The wine has dried,
the drinker's died
and here is the evidence,
the diamond spade delves
for everyday items
new diamonds themselves
to be placed on shelves
for the eyes of the people.
But I am informed that last night
that sight was shortened
as this site of diligent tillage
was unsettled and pillaged,
by pillocks with metal detectors.

Digging for it

Sometimes a poem is less of an invention
and more of a find
its birth a kind
of archaeology,
a job of unearthing and piecing together
and sometimes a piece won't fit
because it's part of something else,
and sometimes it is just a bit of old rubbish.

The pillars of the gods

In the dark ages
the remains of Roman extravagance
must have been a top-most mystery
to a population with such a lack
of building skills
and history teachers.
Who were these beings
with such a miraculous knack
of stacking stones?
Where did they go?
and more unnervingly,
when would they be back?

Sat on the Pillar of Hercules

I bought a book about Roman eroticism
with images and artefacts
the museums had banned,
just for research purposes you'll understand.

Forever Roman

Mile after Roman mile,
travelling from Newcastle to Carlisle,
in spite of seeing Hadrian's Wall
now fallen like the empire,
I imagined a Roman at that Empire's height
standing by the roadside
and seeing the way of the Romans
stretching to a distance
as far as this moment of mine.
A Roman with a future,
for whom the sun was equally high,
under an identical
blue sky.

Gaul

Once a Centurion soldier
said Venus how I want to hold yer
she replied I'm a god
and it's great on my tod
and his mate said Marcellus I told yer.

A centurion has a bit of fun

This centurion goes to a dance and for the first time in ages he lets others take the lead. Like a child with a rattle he is wild and unselfconscious, but the following morning he's rather stiff because him and all his hundred are killed like cattle on the battlefield.

___ The Roman ruins of Chester ___

On the last leg of the journey to Chester on 'The Sprinter' (which is like a sprinter with a bad leg) I see a hill fort and remember that the Romans were at Chester. During the evening's performance I am persistently heckled by a man with his legs over the empty seat in front of him. I point out to him that he is rather unlikeable; the audience seems to be in agreement and cheer menacingly like punters in a gladiatorial amphitheatre.

On leaving the hotel in the morning I have 35 minutes before my train is due to depart. I see a hackney taxi, hail it and tell the driver that I would like him to take me to the railway station, but first could he show me something of Roman Chester? He says there is the Amphitheatre and some Roman gardens and I am most agreeable. The Amphitheatre is rather unspectacular, a single layer of stones, little more than markers of what was once magnificent. But it IS Roman and touching the red stone makes me tingle. As we drive on, my impromptu guide points out the oldest pub in Chester and some Tudor carvings. I feel it would be rude to point out that I am not interested; I want to see Roman things. When he shows me the remnants of an abbey which he says was built before Roman times I do sit up rather and wonder if this can possibly be true. Who built it then? I enquire. The monks before the Romans came, I'm told. No – I think he must have got it wrong. Now these Roman Gardens, can I have a look at them?

He says he will have trouble parking but manages and as I enter the Gardens I pass two men painting the railings in boiler suits. I wonder what the Romans would have made of the scene.

They would probably have understood the paint, possibly some of the dialogue, but I think the boiler suits would have been very surprising. Inside the Gardens is an immense sense of peace and the remains of pillars which remain magnificent. I embrace them and for a momentous minute or so I hold History in my arms, then return to the taxi where I see I have clocked up four hundred and eighty pounds. We drive to the station. I put three quid into the cobbled palm, enter the concourse and buy three copies of a postcard depicting the Roman Garden ruins. On the train I wonder what a Roman might think of the picture. Depends on the Roman of course, but say it was your average sort of bloke, a fairly intelligent painter and decorator say. He might think it was a painting of how the Roman Garden might appear after many centuries. He would obviously not see it as a photograph, the process being unknown. If he were to see a second postcard he would think the hand of a skilful copier was at work; on seeing a third he might become confused; on seeing forty thousand or so he might think you could use them as wallpaper.

The Coliseum

it was difficult to see
if you were sat at the back
it was more difficult
if you needed the kind of spectacles
which were yet to be invented
it was worse if you were the worse for wine
and even worse if you were cursed
with a row of very tall citizens
sat immediately in front
and even worse than that
if your medium-sized master
obtained a better view
by getting you to lie flat on the terrace
so that he could sit on your spine

The Roman showm'n

The Roman showm'n
informs the throng
that he would like it to be noted
that some of his better material is quoted
in the senate
in fact
one of them once asked him to script them a speech
and he said why don't you go and pen it
yourself Julius?
Although he admits to changing his mind later
when it was suggested
that alternatively he might prefer catering
for the lions.

He gets to his gigs in a chariot
just for a bit of display
and he starts with a song
that is reasonably strong
called Rome Wasn't Built in a Volcano.

He's been all around the empire
and around it all again
from Sicilia to Jerusalem
and from Africa to Lutonium.

And he warns if they juggle with too many balls
they'll balls up the whole of the act,
then he stands there and juggles a solitary ball
saying this is how jugglers get sacked.

He's good on the spur of the moment
which is good when the heckling begins
he once told a group of inebriate Christians
how lucky they were that their sins
had already been died for.
This shut them up apparently.

Togas

when togas had gone out of fashion
Augustus tried bringing them back
and the trendier folk in the forum
would joke about people who wore 'em

St George's Day poem

I like old English inns
but not Ye Olde Worlde pretence
I like the Stonehenge circle
so much better than the fence.

I like an English apple
(the bit that's not the core)
I like the little chapel
up on Glastonbury Tor.

I don't like English butchery
I don't like English lamb
verging on the English vegetarian I am
I do like English haddock though
I think it should be said
but do they know they're English fish
especially when they're dead?
No. Oh nonny nonny no they don't.

I like the English countryside
and English country tea
and lots of English mustard
but not in Irish coffee.

I love my English country
and other countries too;
I won't order egg and chips
when I'm in Timbuctoo.
I do like egg and chips though
and sticks of Brighton rock

and when I fry myself an egg
I never use a wok,
do you?
No?
Good.

I like the English language
I like the word latrine,
it's somewhere to express yourself
where others might have been.

I like the English heritage
I like to hear archaic English folk songs
being sung in that distinctive nasal way
but not all day.

Maurice

A dog's complaint

They say a dog's a man's best friend
but not a dog's best friend's a man
it isn't that surprising
when you're only there to guard his van
an inch of wound-down window
it can drive you from your wits,
it's a dog's life.

Sometimes a dog's called Rover
and sometimes he's called Rex
these names they are rubbish
and they're only for a certain sex;
humans like to know you
by the nature of your bits
and the rule is if they match,
you're not to touch each other's privates.

They're glad that we can understand
the substance of their talk,
a shame they think all we can say is
I think there's someone at the door
or master can I have a walkies.
I like it in the open though,
rolling in the grass,
striking up acquaintances
and sniffing fellow creatures up the
trees where they have recently been past.

Haircut in Seville

He guesses that I'm English
and gets on with the job.
Without my spectacles
there is little to see in the mirror
and I reflect on the holiday so far:
the flight, the first day in the hired car
and the fright
from my friend's difficulty remembering
that the traffic in Spain
stays mainly on the right;
November sunbathing in Cadiz
and the business with the prawns
in the mountain town of Rhonda.
as I ponder
the barber
runs his razor round my neck,
I keep very still
and hope he doesn't harbour ill
about the plight of the Armada.

Sketches of Portugal

On the track back
from the ruins of Conimbriga
finding a fraction of exercise book
in familiar looking folds
I wonder about the old Romans again,
did they make parchment aeroplanes?

On the trains
the notices on the windows
say not to throw bottles out,
unlike their English counterparts
which prohibit mere leaning.

On the roads apparently
there are more disasters
than anywhere else in Europe,
on the streets
the boys are selling plasters.

A Barrow escape

My fortune was told me in Barrow
by someone called Old Madame Tarot,
she said danger is near
it was lucky to hear
'cos I ducked
and avoided an arrow,
but Old Madame Tarot wasn't quite so
    fortunate.

On the Isle of Man

On the Isle of Man
remembering that here
it is bad to be gay,
and not within the law,
and I wonder if anyone's made jokes
about entering Douglas before.

Grange-over-Sands

When they had fallen asleep
in the great hotel,
the snow fell.
By the morning it had laid
and after their Cumbrian breakfast
they came out into the quiet flakes
and made
a snow dog.
Although it had no name or bone,
it had its own snowball
and a small snow owner
who seemed to be an infinitely patient man,
and what with the Woodland Walk
and the nearby Lakes
they found themselves agreeing
that it was a very good place
to bring a dog
into being.

Bury St Edmunds

Getting dark near closing
in the park of the abbey ruins
I enter the recreation ground.
It has been raining off and on,
all the children are gone
and I am tempted by the swings,
things I spent hours on
when my trousers went no lower than my knees.
A small go would do no harm I decide.
Settled into the ride
and aware that I am breaking the rules
I prepare for the possible appearance
of a hostile parkie.
Why shouldn't I be here?
I'm no more danger to the apparatus
than ten stone three
of heavyweight child might be!
How strict is the authorised age-range anyway?
If you're one second past fourteen
does that mean you're banned?
And if I had a mental understanding age of nine
maybe that would be fine, would it, eh?
Some way off a figure
rounds the corner with some keys,
before the shape gets any bigger
I spill from the still swinging swing
and scarper for the trees.

A childhood hobby

One of my earliest pieces of poetic inspiration
was giving the game of drenching pieces of
tissue paper in spit then flicking them with
our rulers the name of Flobby Gobby.

First sex

I was about six
the first time my mother told me
how it was bad to play with myself,
but I think she preferred it
to me playing with my sister.

____ Lucky Bags ____

A lot of my small boy's sweet money went on Lucky
   Bags:
a few pastel-coloured edible shapes
that smelt too much of scent,
one or two not too tasty toffees
and the occasional slightly bent sweet cigarette,
the incentive to buy a Lucky Bag was not the sweets.
The attraction was the small toy included in every unit.
Excitedly I would feel the bright paper packaging
seeking insight into the nature of the unknown novelty
getting disappointed if I thought it was a whistle of
   some sort
(which it often was)
but you were purchasing anticipation not realisation;
you handed over your threepence
in the hope of the thing you'd always wanted
even if you never knew what that was
you paid your money because one day
you may be lucky.
For some reason I can clearly recall
one bag in particular,
a Jamboree Bag it was actually
exactly the same concept
but with pictures of boy scouts on the outside:
it's a foggy frosty morning
I've done the feeling around
and it's definitely not a whistle
I rip a thin strip from the top of the bag,
in goes my hand

and slowly
out comes the mysterious gift.
It IS a whistle after all,
would be the easy answer,
but not necessarily true
because now I can no longer remember what I had
I no longer know
how lucky
I was.

___ Scottish country dancing ___

It was something in the delicacy of the footwork
which appealed to me
when I first saw them Scottish country dancing in
    assembly
and although I was a bit of a lad about the school
I knew that I too wanted to do this
so I roped a friend into going along to a lesson in the
    dinner hour
and when the teacher saw that it was us
she said that she sincerely hoped we had not come
    there to be stupid
I insisted that we were there to learn
and begrudgingly she let us join the class
and after a bit our feet began to get the idea
and I got such a thrill
from the thought of learning the skill's secret
I laughed out loud at the pleasure of it
and immediately she turned off the record and said
now get out the pair of you
I knew you'd only come here to be stupid

At home

At fourteen I was not seen
by the others in my form
to be normal.
In a classroom debate
Jonathan Hawkins once created great laughter
by addressing us all
as ladies, gentlemen and Hegley.
But things were different
down behind the goal at Luton Town FC of a
    Saturday afternoon,
my pre-match chatter
mattered as much as anybody's,
belittling schooltime sniggers were no more
this was something bigger than schooltime
and at the entrance of the sacred twelve
swarming after their warm-up footballs
and soon to be put to the test
I was there with the rest
I was one of the crowd
I was part of the roar
LUTON
LUTON
LUTON
urging them to score,
and louder than Jonathan Hawkins.

Plasticine glasses

When my pocket money went up
from threepence
to fourpence,
my Dad referred to the revised figure
as big boys' pocket money.
Before I saw through big boys' glasses
I was to be seen
in glasses made of plasticine;
more colourful and flexible
than my specs are now
and less likely to fly off
when my Dad gave me a jolly good shaking
like he did once
when I was dressed up as a bus conductor.

Sheds

Once more I'm on the tracks
on my way to Hastings
looking at the passing house-backs
and contemplating sheds:
ramshackle sheds
ship-shape sheds
sheds with burglar alarms
surprisingly tall sheds
I-thought-it-was-a-kennel-it's-so-small sheds,
they're all sheds;
except for the greenhouses.
I wonder if the Normans had sheds.
I don't suppose a pair of glasses
would have been much good to Harold
when it came to all the bloodshed.

Can I come down now Dad?

My first memory of the toilet
dates from the beginning of training in its use,
being sat over the bowl
and told that this was where a big boy went to
    the toilet
and not in his potty
and not in a nappy,
and I was unhappy
and I cried and said, 'Daddy I'm scared
I shall fall down the hole!'
But I must have beaten my fear of the toilet
    somehow
because I've never been worried
about falling down the hole since
except once when I was very depressed.

The stand up comedian sits down

the comedian climbs onto the stage
and truthfully points out
that the microphone smells of sick
so does your breath says somebody
get on with it says somebody else
please settle down
replies the comedian responding well
I'll start this routine if it kills me
there is an outbreak of cheering
at the mention of his death
get off says the one who said get on with it
and the comedian comes up with a line
so apt and incisive
that any further heckling is redundant
unfortunately he comes up with it
on the bus home

These Were
Your Father's

A few words about poetry

Adrian Mitchell has suggested that most people ignore most poetry because most poetry ignores most people, to which I would add that most porcupines ignore most putty because putty is usually quite high off the ground and porcupines usually aren't and they tend not to notice things unless they're of an edible, threatening, or sexually attractive nature.

D. H. Lawrence spoke of poetry as that which brings a new attention to something. This is what the Martian poets were after; Craig Raine, through his Martian eye, sees the book as a many-winged bird. Similarly, a pair of glasses might be seen as a bird with no wings, no body, no head and a pair of glasses.

A many-winged rain hat

Holy orders

Be sharp, be blunt,
hunt out the fox
of your own vox popular,
be jocular, be ocular
however much they mocular;
be rigorous, irregular
but don't go being negular,
whip away the rugular
from being smugly smugular,
when going for the jugular
refrain from being ugular:
enlighten and surprise,
put a sparkle in their eyes
and a few quid in your pocket.

Brother Trevor

He handed in his cowl
and his trowel
and took leave of his order for ever,
taking a position as a warder
in an already overcrowded prison.
After the celibate years
being thought of as 'a screw'
took a bit of getting used to
and in spite of having no cell of his own now
he found the new uniform didn't allow
quite as much freedom of movement.

Network SouthEast beast

Benevolent
not malevolent;
after its feast
of commuters,
they are released.

Vision in the tunnel

When you're going through a tunnel on a train
and you look at the wall
it can seem like you're going the other way
and if you want to you can go into a sort of
    dream
and tell yourself
that you really are
and when you come out of the tunnel again
you can feel your brain having a little problem
sorting itself out
but you may think you have enough problems
    already
without worrying about this sort of nonsense.

Consideration

In the crowded compartment
there's a man with a noisy computer game toy.
I'm sure it's not just me he's annoying
but I don't want to confront him alone.
Maybe I should stand up and ask
if anyone else would like him to stop
but maybe they won't answer,
and maybe they'll all take out one of their own.

Stimulation

The first time my brother saw me in action
he explained that he didn't use his hands at all
and demonstrated how he could achieve
   excitement
by merely rubbing his knees together.
I copied his method
as I copied many things my brother did
believing him to be a most exemplary boy
but on this occasion my only reward
was a slight abrasion of the knees.

Was it a coincidence?

Once, I'd chopped up some wood
and afterwards
in the immediate vicinity
I found some wood which had
recently been chopped up.

Light sleep

Early in the evening I like to have a kip
and dip
into the pool of the communal unconscious;
resting, passive,
where whatever size of drip you are
you make the whole
more massive.

That's entertentment

While I was gone away
down to the spray
of the ocean,
leg bent
the dog went
in my tent,
it was a small wet
and yet
it meant
more to me
than all the sea did.

A three-legged friend

They have a three-legged dog
and they call him Clover
and sometimes he falls over
and if he'd have had four legs
maybe they'd have called him
Lucky.

The Cub Scout diary

One Christmas I told my dad
that my sister had scribbled on the pages of my new
   Cub Scout diary.
When he confronted her about the damage
and she pleaded innocent
I asked who did it if she never
and realising there was no other likely suspect,
assuming our parents to be above such a senseless
   violation,
Angela said that although she had no
recollection of the incident
the culprit must have been her;
an admission which my father felt
warranted a thorough beating.
What had actually occurred was
whilst entering my address in the diary,
which I wanted to look as neat as possible,
I had made a mistake,
crossed it out, made a mess
and lost my temper,
ruining the book
with a series of indelible markings.
When the frenzy was over
I decided that somebody should suffer for this act of
   destruction
and that that person should be my sister.

Father Coombes

the old parish priest shows
me the floral feast
of his front garden
pardon my ignorance Father
but what are those?
mahonia
these?
marsh marigolds
and those?
weeds
and those there?
Dicentra spectabilis
he reads
from the little lollystick thing
leaning in the mid-March air
it is spring
and I love it
growth and greenery
and bluery above it
here in winter's hinterland
and here among the blooms
Father Coombes
bollock-naked

Private hire

In the mini-cab
the driver is sneezing
and I want to say 'bless you'
but I feel he wants to keep his distance.

Money well spent

He knew he'd been done but he'd had to have it; he
loved anything old to do with scouting and this book of
camping hints was a real find and the stallholder knew
it. Thirty quid! But he'd had the money and what was
he getting for it? Beauty, antiquity, you couldn't put a
price on that. The date, nineteen twenty-eight, they
knew nothing of a second world war then. The book
was a beautiful orange and not at all faded at the
edges, the staples too were in fine condition, no
additional rust-orange against the inner whiteness of
the pages, but thirty quid was still steep.

There were plenty of the old adverts which he loved,
because the things which they publicised were things
you could no longer buy, the addresses if they still
existed would have gone through many incarnations
since the time of publication, yet the text knew nothing
of this and innocently promised the advertised goods
for a very reasonable and archaic remittance.

He turned to the first page of the scouting material.
Why was it he was so fascinated by scouting? He read
a résumé of the Scout law: 'Trusty, loyal and helpful,
brotherly, courteous, kind, obedient, smiling and
thrifty, and clean in thought, word and mind.' He did
not agree that all the properties listed were qualities
but it was the attempt at a code for right living that
attracted him and it was something the modern world
disowned – well, he didn't. The Boy Scout movement
might be moving towards obsolescence but the
founding concept was sound enough. There was much

good amongst the nonsense: the fetching hats, the wacky salute, the knotting, the yarns, the alertness; he loved it as a boy, he loved it still. He smelt the book and as he did so, he sniffed up the molecules of another age and went into a deep deep reverie like a campfire sleep and he was taken back to a Scout hut somewhere in the nineteen twenties. The book WAS new, and now it had returned to its own time and it had taken its loyal reader with it. The group of Scouts in the middle of whom he had landed were rather surprised, but their skipper had always realised that the circles and rituals were a potent invocation and John set about trying to do good Scout work to challenge the course of history and the troop became his helpers and John had no doubt in his mind that the book had been worth thirty quid.

Man and Gran united

Grandma she was walking
with her dog by the canal
when she recognised a foreign man
who wasn't an Italian,
it was Eric Cantona
he was sitting on a bench
Eric is a football star and Eric's French.
Eric Cantona, Eric Cantona
he likes to kick the ball under the bar
Eric Cantona, Eric Cantona
Grandma's favourite footballer by far.
The dog jumped up on Eric's bench
and Eric said bonjour,
the doggie made an awful stench
and Eric he said eughh!
(but he said it in French).
Grandma said I'm sorry Eric
Eric said c'est la vie
and Grandma thought he said celery.
Then Eric spoke in English
and he asked the doggie's name
and Grandma said I call him Jesus
because he isn't just for Christmas
then the doggie fouled the pavement
and Eric fouled the dog.
Eric Cantona, Eric Cantona
Gérard Depardieu it isn't who you are
Eric Cantona, Eric Cantona
a banana with no ner is a bana.

Where it will all end

If the crime statistics continue to rise
every act will be criminal
and all domestic visitors will be present
solely to size the place up
for the purpose of a burglary.
All street meetings
will end in beatings
and you will be asked if you have the time
only for it to be taken away from you.
Everyone will be on the fiddle always.
All of the youth
will be morally uncouth
thugs on drugs;
all transactions will be theft,
all excursions will be alibis,
there will be nothing left but lies
and I don't believe a word of it.
Here, where's my wallet!

Over the top of the paper

I was sitting in the Sleazy Moon caff reading my paper,
happily immersed in the worst of the latest disasters,
when momentarily, I had a sensation that the news was
    just a blind,
something keeping me from finding something more
    sensational
and not so far away.
Taking a peek over the top of my page
I noticed that the salt, sugar, sauce, and mustard
were all clustered,
keeping away from the pepper
like it was some kind of a leper.
And on the other side of the table I could see
that my tea
was too big, far too big.

The fabric of life

There's a dye to colour a cotton plaster
a certain perky
pink
and the patch will match
some people's skin
but in many cases the mismatch shows
especially on the skin
of potatoes.

Friendship

On this ship of friends
if your heart sank
I would gladly walk the plank
and dive five fathoms
into your sea of troubles.

Deep in shallow waters

Relieving myself in the Mediterranean
it occurs to me that some of my wee
has become part of the wider sea
which triggers thoughts of individuals
who think they're really big
when really they are piddley.

Happy family

Under the sun the dog with a stick
under the dog the woman with thick hair.
Daddy's there with junior,
both have hats and glasses – junior's are small
that's about all
oh, and Father is fond
beyond
the call of beauty.

My father's footwear

Once, a skinhead in my class
came round my house in his Doctor Martens
and passing the rubber galoshes
which my dad wore
to dig the garden
he got me to try them on
and he said 'gosh John,
those galoshes look really smart,
you should start
wearing them into school.'
And foolishly I did.

Valentine's complaint

Apparently the Romans beheaded Saint Valentine for his Christian beliefs, but before his slaughter he sent a message to his jailer's daughter who'd become enamoured in their meetings when she'd brought him his eatings.

Many times love has been declared
and many times such love has died
once it has been shared.
Love can last for ever
if we never speak its name
it seems a shame to thwart it
in a short moment of fame.
Undying loving's precious scraps
are beans we shouldn't spill
but being as I shall soon be dead
I think perhaps I will:
you've been a pal
and golden gal
to this old Valentine,
my heart is yours although my head
will shortly not be mine.
I trust the one I'm off to meet
is equally divine.

Inspector Nostril

To him the faintest odour
has a really pungent reek – I speak of Inspector
  Nostril.
Here is his picture:

He's called Inspector Nostril
because he only has one nostril.
Known as Inspector No Nonsense
to his friends
and Inspector Nonsense to the enemy
he tends to sniff the lower reaches of a suspect
in the way that dogs do
but he gets results.
His beak
is the peak
of his powers
so to speak.

The new member

On her wedding day it rains
rice grains
and she explains
that she has joined the pudding club.

___ Res Romanae (Roman things) ___

When we were sat in Latin
the teacher used to very occasionally break the tension
of verb and noun declension
by getting us to get out
our Res Romanae books for ten minutes or so.
These were little books in which we registered
the Roman proverb and the Roman pun
and things the Romans did for fun
like swimming
and skimming flattish pebbles
discus-like across the sea,
still pretty dull
but we got by
a little better
with Res Romanae – Roman things.

On the long last day of a summer term
the heat indoors made the pupils squirm
and the teacher who was very firm
softened up for once and said
today we shall do something different
and eagerly we started chattin'
imagining some cricket battin' –
a pleasure he would deny,
'for the WHOLE lesson boys,' he told us
'we shall enjoy our Res Romanae.'

—— The Roman teacher ————————

In the Greek lesson
it is the summertime
and this morning is the last time
for two cycles of the moon
that he will commune with his pupils.
Earlier this morning was the last time ever
he would commune with his beloved
for she has fooled around with another
and his jealousy is stronger than his love.
On his arrival some of the pupils are winking at each
    other
thinking that today they will be schooled
without the usual iron glove,
allowed along to the beach
to have a smashing splashing time
swimming and skimming flattish pebbles
discus-like across the sea
but they are wrong.
It is *his* curriculum, *his* anger
and this morning they will share his pain,
they will each take out their tablets
and have a stab at giving six good reasons
why they shouldn't get a thorough thrashing with his
    cane.

On Hadrian's Wall

I imagined local children had a bladder just for
   kicks;
I could see them booting their ball about
down the centuries
and up against the bricks.

Wheelchairs in ancient Rome

Did they lack appropriate access?
Did the stacked steps
consistently cause despair?

Not if yours was the Emperor's wheelchair.

No credit

The pyramids are a wonder
but we're left to wonder who
the brickies were who did the job,
there must have been a few
of them, mustn't there?

And the Bible names the wiseguys
with the frankincense and myrrh
but who knows who
the shepherds were?

They didn't get a credit.
They got lost in the edit.

Egg cosy

Before its head is splitted
the egg is fitted
with knittedness,
before the silver smash
a moment's fashion
consciousness.

Fireside fun

When we had an open fire
my dad used to hate
me sitting in the fireplace
or the grate as he would refer to it.
He used to say he couldn't feel the benefit
of the fire
but one day I made a pledge
to stay out on the edge
and the room was decorated with smiles
as I demonstrated how I could keep within the
    confines
of the first half-dozen tiles
and won over by the humour
my father made them mine
and in the future he referred to them
as John's six squares
and sometimes he allowed me
to have nine.

Hospital art

In the afternoons, between toileting
the doubly incontinent patients
and giving them their tea
there were a couple of hours
in which the staff and patients usually sat around
    staring into space.
I might have been the same after a few years in the place
but being an enthusiastic newcomer
and a student on vacation
I said hey, let's get everybody doing art!
So I got the materials we needed,
sat everyone around tables and proceeded.
They were not the most capable of artists
but together we made some things which put up on the
    wall together
really brightened up the ward.
The next day I was not working
and on my return I found the walls to be bare.
The staff nurse had torn down the pictures;
he told me they were ugly
and they underlined the inabilities of the patients.
I said that the pictures had gone
because they were a reminder
of the fact that he spent the afternoons staring into
    space
rather than trying to do something creative
with those in his care.
I said he was a disgrace.
I said I hope you're very proud,
but I never said it aloud.

My father's pullover

My father was older than other dads
and when I was fifteen or so
I used to call him 'old man'.
When I was younger such abuse
would have triggered prolific use
of the back of his hand
but I think he thought me too old and too big for that
    now,
not that he was cowardly,
I got the feeling that he was prepared
to square up to any aggressor
but a full-scale physical to-do with his adolescent son
would have given him a sense of parental failure.
I remember that in his frustration with my insolence
he would involuntarily pull down the bottom of his
    sleeveless pullover
which I would imitate
to make his frustration greater.

The young poet

The first time I wrote in verse
I was about ten,
I wrote about my den
and someone said it's like a real poem Miss
and Miss said it is a real poem, John.
I've been a poet since then.

The Weekender

I once went on what was called a Weekender in a hotel
up in Grange-over-Sands. I'd seen them advertised
when I was doing a show in the area. I took the train
up there; it was at the very beginning of the mobile
phone boom, and for the whole journey there were
three separate people on and off these infernal
machines and that was just at my table. To be truthful,
when I say the whole journey I only mean the Inter-
City part from London to Lancaster. At Lancaster I
had to change to a local train on which I was
accompanied by two of the mobile maniacs, whom I
avoided by parking myself in a separate compartment
where electronic game machines seemed to be the
thing.

I object to mobile phones on trains because they are
an imposition of something private in a public area,
usually by people who kick up a right old stink if the
transgression is the other way round.

Arriving in Grange-over-Sands I popped down into
the town to get myself some condoms 'just in case',
then made my way up the hill to the hotel. In the foyer
there was a huge dog, a Great Dane I think, which
moved about with difficulty. The person at the
reception desk spoke familiarly with the dog and had
an intriguing toupee. After receiving my key and
Weekender welcoming letter, I took my duffle bags up
the grand Victorian staircase to my room, number One-
ten. To my delight I was at the front of the hotel with a
wonderful view of the gardens and greenery beyond.

To my dismay I discovered rather a lot of dog muck in the bathroom. After reporting my discovery I was apologetically moved to the room next door, number One-eleven, which had an equally enchanting view but from a slightly different angle. I settled down to enjoy my welcoming letter. 'Dear guest', it began disappointingly, but then the text went on less formally, inviting me for drinks with all the other guests at 6.30 p.m. Great, I thought, that's in half an hour from now.

After a quick sort-out and shower I made my way down the grand old Victorian staircase to face my fellow Weekenders. I was to discover that they were all at the senior citizen end of the age spectrum apart from two young people jabbering into their mobiles, whom I decided to ignore, introducing myself instead to a lively older woman who was talking to the hotel dog.

We got chattering and I discovered that she shared my interest in railway travel and the television programme *Blockbusters*. Our conversation was curtailed when she went up to bed at eight o'clock, but not before we had agreed to take the train to Barrow-in-Furness the following morning. For the remainder of the evening I chatted with the dog.

Upstairs I mixed up my complimentary cup of cocoa and relaxed reflectively in my complimentary armchair. It hadn't been the best birthday I'd had but it certainly wasn't the worst. It was certainly the second worst though, I argued with myself. 'Stop your moaning and turn on the telly.' I did as I was ordered and suddenly I perked up; they were advertising a new programme called *Bob's Your Uncle* and for a moment I thought this referred to Bob Holness the quizmaster in *Blockbusters*, but it didn't.

However the night saw a tall fall of snow which considerably increased my relish for the next day's outing. Dora understandably greeted the sight of the white with less enthusiasm on account of her greater brittleness of bone. However, we made our way down to the station without mishap and happily sat reading our respective morning papers as we awaited the ten o'clock from Preston. I said to Dora that it was a very good sign if people felt relaxed enough to sit reading things together and Dora said she'd appreciate it if I didn't interrupt her while she was reading and she'd prefer it if I called her Mrs Phelps. She didn't speak to me again until we were arriving in Barrow and that was only to ask me to swap papers. Fortunately there was nothing in mine which took her fancy and we had a comprehensive look around the shops, a long leisurely sit in the caff with some books we'd purchased and a gorgeous journey back in the twilight snow, marred only by a couple of interruptions from Mrs Phelps's mobile phone.

To be continued

Tea and turps

You stepped into the café
then you sat down next to me
I'd just ordered breakfast
and you were my cup of tea.
You said pass the sugar
and you passed the time of day
I said it was lovely
although it was really grey.
I said do you live round here
and you asked me my name
then I asked what yours was
and they were not the same.
You said you painted portraits
and you'd like a go at mine
you said come up to my studio
and be my turpentine.

Pat's paintings

Who's this then Pat?
It's my father.
What's his eye doing down there?
That's his mouth.
What's this then?
That's the Oval cricket ground.
Looks more oblong to me. What's that brown
    thing?
My mother's dog.
And who's that oblong woman, your mother?
Yes it is.
What's her eye doing down there??
That's her vagina.

The customer's complaint

In the caff
swapping some of her spaghetti
for a bit of his moussaka
she considered what a benefit it was having a
    partner
when you both wanted the same two
separate meals on the menu.
Unfortunately she considered it
to be the only benefit.

Not very independent

Picking up the paper
I cannot believe the headline.
It has nothing to do
with the argument we had this morning.
Spreading through the home news
still nothing about our domestic blitz,
the bits of sports are the athletic
not the spiteful sort;
the Arts page: no art of deception;
the Science section?
nothing of the scientific reproach;
'Business' is business as usual,
the crosswords are cryptic rather than crass,
the horoscope alas
it alludes, but doesn't broach.
Finally I approach
the obituaries
and give them my attention with dread:
fortunately there is no mention
of love being dead.

Past perfection

You used to be
my cup of tea
but now you're not so hot,
you couldn't see
enough of me
but now you see the lot.
It used to be a mystery
but now it's only us,
once you were my cup of tea
but now you're more like pus.

Table talk

SALT. Just because you've got loads of holes you think you're special.

PEPPER. No I don't I just think I'm fortunate.

SALT. You do, you really think you're better than me don't you?

PEPPER. No, I've just got more holes.

SALT. You can't stop can you?

PEPPER. Look, it's just how it is. I've never actually counted my holes you know. OK what have I got, seven, eight maybe, and you've got one. But in the whole world there are millions of holes and compared to that we're both insignificant.

SALT. You patronising cruet. I'm leaving you for the vinegar.

PEPPER. Suit yourself but it's only got one hole.

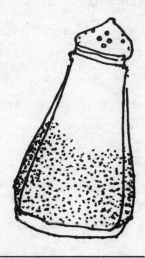

Poetry in India

I'm in India,
feeling more secure
and less likely to get chinned 'ere.
I made friends with a steam-train fireman
who asked how long I would stay in his country.
'Two weeks,' I replied.
'Very short?' he probed.
'I'm a very busy man,' I joked.
'What is it, the work you do?' he probed further.
'Poetry!' I announced.
'Aha!' he pounced,
'Now I understand you,
my brother does the same.
Yes, very hard work:
the feeding, the cleaning, loading all the eggs on
    to the lorry.'

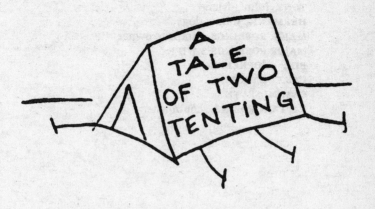

Characters

JOHN
TONY, John's friend
HERMANN, John's dog
MAJOR ROBBINGS, campsite owner
MAJOR ROBBINGS'S WIFE
BIKE-SHOPKEEPER
CAB CONTROL
GEMINI SEVEN
CAPTAIN ROBINS, scoutmaster

JOHN. This time tomorrow we'll have tents to go to, Tony.

TONY. Two teas please Harry. You're all sorted then?

JOHN. A nice weak one for me please Harry, yeah I'm all sorted. I'm having to improvise a bit but I'm all sorted. I've safety-pinned a couple of blankets together ...

TONY. Why don't you buy a sleeping bag?

JOHN. I've got a sleeping bag Tony, the blankets are my tent. I've safety-pinned two big blankets together and gaffa-taped some polythene sheeting to the blankets.

TONY. What about a groundsheet?

JOHN. That's what the polythene sheeting's for.

TONY. But what about the outside of the tent?

JOHN. The weather forecast didn't say anything about rain.

TONY. It did.

JOHN. Have you got an umbrella?

TONY. I've got five.

JOHN. Can I have one?

TONY. You can have four if you want. At what point do you put an umbrella up John? You can tell a lot about a person from whether they do it at the first tiny inkling of rain or wait until everybody else is doing it.

JOHN. When do you put yours up?

TONY. I like to be last.

JOHN. I like to be about seventh. Are you taking anything to read?

TONY. Just this.

JOHN. Mm ... *The Scoutmaster's Manual*. Sounds like fun.

TONY. It says you need to take a hurricane light John, you've got a torch on your key-ring though, that'll do. How's the light of your love life, anyway?

JOHN. It's all over, Tone. The new beginning ended up the same as the old one. I'm emotionally derelict apparently.

TONY. How about tent pegs?

JOHN. I was going to use biros.

Hey Tone, you don't mind if I take my dog along?

TONY. What dog?

JOHN. The one made out of an old potato sack.

TONY. Bring him along.

JOHN. Here Tone, do you know how he felt when he found out that he was a puppet? ... gutted.

TONY. No he never, John, but bring him along anyway.

On the road

TONY and JOHN.
We're cycling along
cycling along
singing our we're going camping song.

JOHN.
My name isn't Tony
his name isn't John
our friend's name is camping
camping's champion.

TONY.
Camping is bewitching
and it's life enriching.

JOHN.
> We're champing for some camping
> and itching for tent-pitching
> and our camping kitching.
> The wheels go round
> the ground goes by,
> we're going camping, why?

TONY.
> Because we love it.

JOHN.
> We're going camping, why?

TONY.
> Because it's great.

JOHN *and* TONY.
> We're cycling along
> cycling along
> and singing our we're going camping song.

At the gate

TONY. Hello, Major Robbings? Tony McKenna – I rang you and reserved a spot on the campsite.

MAJOR ROBBINGS. Hello there, McKenna, well you've got the whole place to yourselves at the moment.

TONY. Thanks.

JOHN. Thanks a lot, I'm John by the way and this is my dog.

MAJOR ROBBINGS. No dogs I'm afraid.

JOHN. It's all right he's not real.

MAJOR ROBBINGS. He's not real what?

JOHN. Not real, Sir.

MAJOR ROBBINGS. A dog made out of potato sack is still a dog of some description and dogs of any description are not allowed on this site.

TONY. That's a bit tough isn't it?

MAJOR ROBBINGS. I'm playing by the book.

TONY. Yes but who wrote the book?

MAJOR ROBBINGS. On this occasion it was me.

TONY. Which gives you the right to cross things out.

MAJOR ROBBINGS. Very irregular.

JOHN. Please!

MAJOR ROBBINGS. Please what?

JOHN. Please let me bring my dog in Sir, he won't bark or annoy the other campers because there aren't any and here's ten quid.

MAJOR ROBBINGS. Any noise though and I'll confiscate him; what breed is he?

JOHN. Sack Russell.

MAJOR ROBBINGS. Very good. Name?

JOHN. Hermann Hessian Sir.

MAJOR ROBBINGS. As in Hermann Hesse, the author?

JOHN. Yes Sir.

MAJOR ROBBINGS. No Germans on site I'm afraid.

JOHN. He's from West Yorkshire.

MAJOR ROBBINGS. Ah, my wife's heard of West Yorkshire; all right boys but any noise out of him and you'll be without a dog in your camping. Comprendo?

JOHN *and* TONY. Fully comp. Major!

TONY. Do you want to pitch camp straight away or shall we get the campfire going first?

JOHN. Doesn't feel right having a campfire with no camp, Tone.

TONY. You're right occasionally John and this is one of those occasions.

JOHN. Where's the mallet?

TONY. I think it's in the trailer along with the chairs.

JOHN. Why did you bring the chairs, Tony?

TONY. Well it's not to detract from the experience of camping with extraneous domestic luxuries if that's what you think.

JOHN. No I was just wondering ...

TONY. ALL RIGHT JOHN. Let's not fall out over this. Chair one is firewood for tonight so we don't have to go looking for campfire wood in the dark. Chair two has a hole in the seat to provide a lavatorial facility: a little tip I picked up from *The Scoutmaster's Manual*, which refers to this convenience as 'the chair of leisure'.

JOHN. Gotcha, Tone.

TONY. Good, John. Do you want to use the mallet first?

JOHN. It's not very sharp is it Tone?

TONY. That's because it's a mallet John.

JOHN.

> Knocking them in knocking them in
> Knocking the tent pegs in.
> They may be only biros, but I still knock 'em in.

Hey Tone, why do you think there's so much unpleasantness in the world?

TONY. Lack of communication and lack of community

and the like I'd say.

JOHN. What do you think of pub quizzes; they're pretty good communal exercises aren't they?

TONY. Not bad, not bad. I suppose it depends how much people are playing to win, rather than playing to play.

JOHN. Mm ... I reckon the campfire takes some beating; especially as an elemental experience:

> in the air
> on the earth
> in the presence of fire
> drinking water – in the form of cocoa
> and expressing the fifth element
> the human element
> the ability to laugh, sing and be surprised.

TONY. John?

JOHN. Tone?

TONY. Hurry up with the mallet ...

JOHN. We could have the best of both you know.

TONY. What, you mean a campfire quiz? OK I'll map out some questions.

JOHN. What shall I do?

TONY. Do as you're told John.

The minor campfire

JOHN. It's weird how it seems destructive to burn a chair intact but it doesn't if it's all chopped up.

TONY. It would have been easier to burn as well if we'd

chopped it up as well.

JOHN. So why didn't we Tone?

TONY. Because it's more memorable this way, more remarkable.

JOHN. It's a shame we had to put petrol on it to get it going.

TONY. Yes and it's a shame your tent never went up in flames as well.

JOHN. That's not very pleasant.

TONY. Sorry John, I just find your tent a bit depressing.

JOHN. But where would I be without it? You wouldn't want me in yours would you?

TONY. No – all right John. Let's get on with the quiz.

JOHN. So where would I be without it eh? Tell me that will you?

TONY. OK John, I'm glad your tent never went up with the chair.

JOHN. Thanks Tone. Isn't it great to be away from the phone Tone? Humanity's developed its machines but not itself if you ask me.

TONY. You're right John. People still don't talk to each other on the underground and 4-3-3 was the beginning of the end if you ask me.

JOHN. What's 4-3-3?

TONY. A system for playing football if you ask me.

JOHN. I didn't know that: separate worlds you see Tone we're all living in separate worlds. Back home when I let the dog out, he goes straight over the fence and rolls about in the garden with the neighbour's dog. And do you know what, I don't even know that neighbour's name. We never speak, let alone smell each other's privates.

TONY. Yes but dogs are useless at football John. Let's have the campfire quiz now, are you ready?

JOHN. Ready.

TONY. Question one. Who won the FA Cup in 1956?

JOHN. A football team.

TONY. Correct. Question two, who won the FA Cup in 1957?

JOHN. Another football team.

TONY. Correct. Question three, who won the FA Cup in 1958?

JOHN. Not a team of dogs of any description?

TONY. Correct. And question four, who won the FA Cup in 1959?

JOHN. Nottingham Forest.

TONY. Well done John, you get all the questions right and your prize is to say what's happened to the campfire.

JOHN. It's gone out.

TONY. Correct again John. Time to hit the sack.

JOHN. And time for the Sack Russell to hit the sack too. Sleep tight on the slight slope Tope.

TONY. Good night John.

Day Two

TONY. Good morning John. Here's a cup of tea for you.

JOHN. What time is it?

TONY. Quarter past six.

JOHN. What did you wake me up for?

TONY. To give you your tea.

JOHN. Good morning Hermann, how did you sleep?

HERMANN. Lying down on my side.

JOHN. Well I'm glad you weren't lying on my side, it was uncomfortable enough as it was.

TONY. We've got company John. Look it's Major Robbings.

MAJOR ROBBINGS. Yes it's me. I told you what would happen if that dog made a noise. He spoke, so I'm confiscating him.

JOHN. Fair enough.

TONY. We've got more company as well John.

JOHN. Oh yeah, who's that?

TONY. Up there, look; by the wood.

JOHN. Oh, hi ... HI, HELLO THERE! Who are they?

TONY. Dibby and Dobby from Derby, John. A bit of company on the campsite. Makes more of a jamboree of it. Toast, John?

JOHN. Yes, four slices please. So what's the plan for this morning?

TONY. Collecting firewood for tonight, putting up the campfire and cleaning our bikes.

JOHN. That's not much fun!

TONY. All right we'll clean each other's bikes and then we'll have a game of frisbee.

JOHN. We haven't got a frisbee.

TONY. We'll use a stick.

JOHN. Hermann'll enjoy that. Good dog!

TONY. He's gone John.

JOHN. Gone!

TONY. Major Robbings just took him.

JOHN. Oh ... oh yes, I'm not quite with it. I didn't sleep at all well actually.

TONY. Why not?

JOHN. I was using my saddle and bike-lights as a pillow.

TONY. Why's that?

JOHN. To make sure nobody nicked them of course!

TONY. Who?

JOHN. What about those other campers?

TONY. You didn't know they were there.

JOHN. I did.

TONY. You never.

JOHN. I did – I intuited it.

TONY. They don't seem much like bicycle thieves.

JOHN. And they might not be. And maybe they're not whole bicycle thieves but just a little bit of someone's bike – could be tempting couldn't it, just a little bit – like a back light for instance!

Never trust someone you don't know Tony. Simple straightforward advice.

TONY. I'm going to brush my teeth John.

JOHN. What about the toast?

TONY. I've brushed that already.

___ *In the wood* _____

TONY. Right John, before you start chopping let me tell you what *The Scoutmaster's Manual* says about the burning properties of wood, OK?

Ash – the best of all burning woods
Beech – very good
Cedar – good
Elder – useless
Hazel – steady
Larch – good tinder but otherwise disappointing
Oak – slow but steady

JOHN. What sort of tree is this one, Tone?
TONY. No idea John, cut some down anyway and just
remember the basic rules of axe-safety: cut into the
wood rather than the self and never chop a leaning stick.

Back at the camp

JOHN. I don't believe it, my doss bag's gone. Let's have
a look in your tent. I don't believe it, your doss bag's
gone as well!
TONY. But who'd want a couple of old doss bags?
JOHN. The other campers of course.
TONY. But they wouldn't have come camping without
doss bags.
JOHN. Haven't you ever heard of extra warmth?
TONY. Yes I have actually.
JOHN. Well that's what I reckon they've gone for.
Come on Tony.

TONY. Don't be too hasty John, knock first.

JOHN. All right.

TONY. And use some discretion, please John!

JOHN. Of course. Ah excuse me, our sleeping arrangements have disappeared. You haven't stolen them by any chance have you? No? Well you don't mind if we inspect your tent then. Some other thieves might have hidden them behind some of your effects.

TONY. Look, I'm sorry you two but John's a bit upset. ... Share your sleeping arrangements!? You mean lie beside you inside your tent!?!

I don't know – John? Dibby and Dobby have kindly offered to share their sleeping arrangements with us.

JOHN. Well – I don't want any hanky-panky for sure. I've had enough trouble in that department, but being as we're arrangementless the offer is very welcome to me. I'll just go and get some condoms.

JOHN. Get me a couple as well while you're down there would you John ...?

JOHN. Hello everyone, I'm back. Hey Tone, our sleeping arrangements haven't disappeared after all. I'm sorry you two. I remember, I had my eyes shut when I looked in our tents because I only wanted to see what I expected to see.

TONY. Why don't you come to our encampment, we've got a tent each that you could share.

JOHN. Yes, come on down.

TONY. Yes, bring that transistor radio as well if you want.

JOHN. I've got one just like that ... hold on ... oh you were just borrowing it, without permission, fine, fine.

TONY. Here's our tents, treat them like your own.

JOHN. We've just got to clean our bikes and have a game of frisbee with a stick then we'll be right with you.

_____ *After the night with the other campers* _

TONY. Hey John, Dobby's gone.

JOHN. So's Dibby.

TONY. So's their tent.

JOHN. So's yours, Tone.

TONY. At least we've still got the bikes.

JOHN. It's a shame the wheels have gone though.

TONY. We'll have a hike into town to get some more.

JOHN. Maybe Major Robbings will give us a lift. At least they haven't touched the frisbee.

_____ *Up at the gatehouse* _____

TONY. Hello there, is Major Robbings in?

MAJOR ROBBINGS'S WIFE. I'm Major Robbing's wife, the Major's just gone into town to sell a couple of bicycle wheels, can I help you?

JOHN. Oh, we just wondered if there was any chance of a lift into town to get a couple of new wheels for our bikes.

MAJOR ROBBINGS'S WIFE. Tut. He could have sold you his and saved you all a journey.

JOHN. But they might not have fitted!

MAJOR ROBBINGS'S WIFE. Oh they would, the other

campers stole them from you two and sold them to the Major this morning.

JOHN. Oh right.

MAJOR ROBBINGS'S WIFE. Anyway, come in for a cuppa?

JOHN. Hello Hermann, how have they been treating you?

HERMANN. With creosote.

JOHN. Really!

HERMANN. And they keep calling me Sheddie.

MAJOR ROBBINGS'S WIFE. This is the living room, you two . . .

JOHN. Excuse me, have you been creosoting my dog?

MAJOR ROBBINGS'S WIFE. I beg your pardon!! . . . As I was saying this is the living room which doubles as a dog-creosoting parlour, now sit yourselves down and I'll bring you both a bowl of water.

TONY. Tea for me please Mrs Robbings.

MAJOR ROBBINGS'S WIFE. Sorry I was getting confused. Oh and I'd prefer it if you referred to me as Major Robbings's wife. Biscuits?

JOHN. Dog biscuits are they?

MAJOR ROBBINGS'S WIFE. No – ship's biscuits, very nice actually – you're in luck.

JOHN. We're not – you've immobilised our bicycles, you've confiscated our dog and you've covered him in creosote.

MAJOR ROBBINGS'S WIFE. No-no that was my husband. Try not to tar us with the same accusations if you don't mind. His life is his, mine is not. A joint bank account doesn't necessarily mean a joint life. He has done you disservice, I am offering you hospitality. We're different people. We do different things. I'll be right back with the biscuit barrel.

JOHN. OK Tone, after we've biscuited I'll go into town and get some replacement bike wheels – you look after what's left of the gear. I'd better get a cab back; what a drag. A cab on a camping holiday. Do you know what I hate about cars, Tone?

TONY Yes John.

JOHN. Right, well make sure no one drives one over my tent, it's ours now, amico brother!

TONY. Allegro, John.

Back on the road

JOHN.

> I'm hiking along
> hiking along
> singing my not going cycling song.

In the shop

JOHN. Hello there, those two secondhand bicycle wheels in the window please.

SHOPKEEPER. Oh yes, I only just got them in this morning.

JOHN. Actually I recognise those reflectors, I think they were stolen from my friend and me yesterday.

SHOPKEEPER. I'm sorry to hear that sir; I can do you a trade discount on them and shall I call you a taxi – it'll be easier than walking back to the campsite with them.

JOHN. That's very kind of you, thanks; you can always rely on the cycling community.

CONTROL. Base to Gemini Seven. Where are you Gemini Seven?

GEMINI SEVEN. I'm just POB.

CONTROL. OK. Tell me when you're clear.

JOHN. So how come you're picking up in a nine-seater?

GEMINI SEVEN. That's all they had left.

... Look at that, do you see that, no indicator or nothing? Now I'm not the world's greatest driver ...

JOHN. Nor is he, eh?

GEMINI SEVEN. Eh ... No.

CONTROL. Gemini Seven.

GEMINI SEVEN. Yeah?

CONTROL. Did your last fare give you a Roman coin by mistake?

GEMINI SEVEN. What?

CONTROL. A Roman coin in the money she gave you?

GEMINI SEVEN. She gave me a fiver.

CONTROL. OK Gemini Seven, tell me when you're clear, I've got another job waiting.

JOHN. Oh look – there's a bank with a thatched roof – they're not very common, are they?

GEMINI SEVEN. Don't suppose they are.

JOHN. My dad used to like thatched buildings.

GEMINI SEVEN. Yeah? – Anyway feel free to smoke. Where are you going with those bike wheels then?

JOHN. Back to the campsite – the bloke who runs the campsite nicked them and sold them off in the town – and he confiscated the dog and covered him in creosote.

GEMINI SEVEN. Yeah? – no respect some people.

JOHN. How long have you been mini-cabbing then?

GEMINI SEVEN. Twenty minutes, you're my second job. I think we're going the wrong way, sorry about that mate, I'll knock it off the fare.

JOHN. We should be all right. It's not that big this town, is it?

GEMINI SEVEN. It's big enough when you don't know where you're going.

JOHN. My dad got a cab once ...

CONTROL. Gemini Seven ...

GEMINI SEVEN. Hold on mate.

CONTROL. Gemini Seven: She says she definitely paid you the fare in coin.

GEMINI SEVEN. She's mistaken.

CONTROL. But she's a regular, Gemini Seven.

JOHN. Fancy that, a Roman coin; fancy someone having a Roman coin loose in their pocket.

GEMINI SEVEN. Don't you start. She gave me a fiver.

CONTROL. Gemini Seven!

GEMINI SEVEN. I'm sorry love but I'm bringing the bus back to base after this job; it's doing my head in. I wouldn't mind mate but I'm a Taurus!!

Back at the camp

JOHN. Here we are Tone, two bicycle wheels astonishingly similar to the two that departed.

TONY. A Scouter's Name John.

JOHN. What's that Tone?

TONY. It's a sub-heading in *The Scoutmaster's Manual*

about what to call your scoutmaster. While you've
been gone I've been thinking that we ought to know
where we stand on this camp. We need it to be clear
who's the troop and who the troop leader is. Troop
alert troop alert!

Right John, 'A Scouter's Name: Friendly relations
won't be built up if the Scouter is addressed as Mister.
Some prefer Sir but others feel this is too formal. In
many troops the name Skipper or Skip is favoured
because it is both respectful and friendly.'

JOHN. Why can't I combine Skip and Tone and call you
Scone, Tone? Or Scoppy?

TONY. How about Sceptical, John. Just skip the lip will
you?

JOHN. Skorry.

TONY. OK John, I want to get an early night tonight.
We're sharing tent-space on account of the theft
remember.

JOHN. What about the campfire, Skip?

TONY. I've told you, I need some kip. I want to get a grip
on the zip of my sleeping arrangement.

In the tent

JOHN. Hey Skip, are you asleep yet?
TONY. I'm not asleep John.
JOHN. Nor me. Hey, did you ever camp in the garden
when you were a kid, Skip?

TONY. You don't have to call me Skip when we're not in uniform John.

JOHN. We haven't got any uniforms.

TONY. A uniform is more than something supplied by an outfitters, John, it's something inside the head, anyway we didn't have a garden.

JOHN. *We* did – but I wasn't allowed to camp in it.

TONY. Why not?

JOHN. We didn't have a tent.

TONY Did you ever go camping with the Scouts?

JOHN. Not in the garden. In a field I did. I remember lying there not being able to sleep, like now, it was the first time I hadn't slept in the same room as my brother.

TONY. I used to sleep with *two* brothers.

JOHN. It was all right, wasn't it?

TONY. What, sleeping with my brothers? I used to tell my big brother to put his socks outside the door because they stank.

JOHN. And did he?

TONY. Yes, but when I was asleep he went and got them and put them under my pillow.

JOHN. When I was very small I had the same furry toys that my brother once had. I built up a really intense relationship with them.

TONY. What did you have?

JOHN. I had a dog, a lion and a giraffe. What did you have?

TONY. Some socks.

JOHN. What did you call them?

TONY. Smelly.

JOHN. Have you ever been scared of the dark, Tone?

TONY. Only once.

JOHN. When was that?

TONY. That time a burglar walked into my room.

JOHN. Horrible. It makes me scared just thinking of it.

TONY. And me.

JOHN. Ooh I'm feeling a bit jumpy. Do you mind if I put the torch on?

TONY. Put it on John.

JOHN. Do you remember Jane who I used to fancy at school?

TONY. Yeah. Don't shine it on me though John.

JOHN. Sorry Tone, do you remember when you and Wojtek held me down so she could kiss me?

TONY. Why did you struggle so much if you fancied her?

JOHN. I don't know, but do you know what?

TONY What John?

JOHN. The one thing in my life that I regret, that I never let her kiss me. I remember her hair dangling in my face.

TONY. It was quite short hair if I remember, she must have been close then.

JOHN. Oh she was close Tone. It's funny, I told Pat about it once and there was no jealousy, even though I said I wanted that kiss like I've never wanted one since.

TONY. It's unthreatening that's why; because you were kids and she wouldn't see a kid from decades ago as competition. Anyway she's left you now and you can kiss who you like.

JOHN. Yeah, but there's a lot to be said for persevering with a relationship.

TONY. How can you persevere if she's left you? You're talking nonsense now, John. Lights out. Come on.

JOHN. Oh Tone, I was enjoying that chat.

TONY. Skipper, John, there's a lot of work to be done in the morning.

JOHN. But you said I could call you Tone.

TONY. No, I'm in uniform now.

JOHN. Good night Skip.

TONY. Good night Patrol Leader.

JOHN. Thanks Skip.

Day Three

TONY. Troop troop alert!

JOHN. What time is it?

TONY. A quarter past five, there's firewood to be gathered John. The woodland awaits.

JOHN. What are you going to do Skip?

TONY. I'm going to expect you not to interrogate your superior officer, John.

JOHN. Fair do's Skipper.

TONY. OK. Stand easy lad.

JOHN. But I'm lying down Skip.

TONY. Skip the quips, John, and get gathering.

Gathering again

JOHN. Oh hello Major Robbings's wife. What are you up to?

MAJOR ROBBINGS'S WIFE. Just walking the old legs.

JOHN. How's my dog?

MAJOR ROBBINGS'S WIFE. YOUR dog? I do find it funny

the way people speak of owning a dog when most of them don't even own themselves. Are the bikes all right now?

JOHN. Yes, but no thanks to your husband.

MAJOR ROBBINGS'S WIFE. I did explain that my husband's business is his own.

JOHN. I've accepted that.

MAJOR ROBBINGS'S WIFE. But you still seem to assume that I share responsibility for him, don't you? I don't. And nor do I desire him.

JOHN. That's no business of mine.

MAJOR ROBBINGS'S WIFE. Everybody's business is everybody else's. Especially in this case because I want to share your sleeping bag, John.

JOHN. That's a bit personal, isn't it? What would your husband think?

MAJOR ROBBINGS'S WIFE. I don't know; hold on I'll call him on the portable and find out ... hello Roger ... I'm with one of the campers ... the one who brought the dog ... yes that's right, the bloke with the dodgy eyesight ... he wants to know what you think about my desire to get inside his sleeping bag ... yes ... yes ... OK thanks Rodge I'll tell him.

   He says he thinks you're obsessed with ownership. And for once he's right, YOUR dog MY husband HIS wife ...

JOHN. But they *were* our saddle bags he had off us.

MAJOR ROBBINGS'S WIFE. Don't you mean bicycle wheels?

JOHN. Yes, I do mean bicycle wheels but I felt like saying saddle bags. You criticise my obsession with ownership but you're obsessed with a world correctly labelled.

MAJOR ROBBINGS'S WIFE. I think you're probably better off in your sleeping bag on your own John. You're afraid of something aren't you?

JOHN. Yes, getting burgled,
getting covered in creosote,
getting poked in the eye with an umbrella ...

MAJOR ROBBINGS'S WIFE. ... getting emotionally involved in someone else's life.

JOHN. Breaking the zip on my sleeping bag ...

MAJOR ROBBINGS'S WIFE. All right John, I'm-a-going, any message for the dog?

JOHN. Yes. Bite.

After the second gathering

TONY. Put it down over there, over there in that rectangle I've marked out with string, that's to be the wood area. Things have got to change around here John.

JOHN. I've just met Major Robbings's wife, Tone.

TONY. SKIPPER!

JOHN. Don't you want to hear about it?

TONY. Don't you want to hear about it, SKIPPER?

JOHN. Sorry Skip, I met her in the wood and she said she wanted to get into my sleeping bag and her husband wouldn't mind ...

TONY. ... I'm sorry John, I don't enjoy having to punch one of my scouts in the face, but if you're going to talk filth like that ...

JOHN. I'm sorry Skipper.

TONY. All right lad, stand easy! OK that's long enough.
    Troop troop alert. Duty Patrol – latrine duty.
JOHN. But Skip we haven't got any latrines.
TONY. Yet. We haven't got any latrines yet.

___ *Troop Two* ___

TONY. Keep digging John.
JOHN. Hey, look! Skip, more visitors. Look Skip, it's a real
    Scout troop!
TONY. No more real than ours, John. Just larger. I think
    I'd like a word with their scouter.
JOHN. What abouter?
TONY. About a merger. Go and ask him to come and have
    a word, would you?

TONY. So what do you think, Captain Robins?
CAPTAIN ROBINS. At the risk of sounding uncourteous, Sir,
    I think you're round the bend and I certainly have no
    intention of putting my troop under the command of
    anybody else, even if they have been appropriately
    invested which I'd hazard you haven't. Now if you
    don't mind I've got some latrine-digging to supervise.
TONY. Pay no heed to him, John, he's a megalomaniac.
JOHN. Oh, can't we make an effort to be friends with
    them, their campfire will be the real thing, with a big
    pow-wow power circle and people doing turns and
    everything, Tone?
TONY. Skipper!
JOHN. It's no good, Tone. Come on let's admit what we

are and make the most of it.

TONY. We're two fish in a little bowl aren't we? And if we make an effort there's a whole ocean out there for us to go and grow bigger in. Sometimes you've got to give up a bit of power to get where you want to be, haven't you. I do see. I was wrong John and it's important to be able to admit you're wrong; we should ask if we can join them.

JOHN. As long as we're part of the movement that's what matters. I'm sure he'll allow you to call him Skipper.

TONY. I'll have to swallow a lot of pride.

JOHN. You can wash it down with campfire cocoa. Come on Tony, major campfire here we come!

Packing up

JOHN. That campfire was a grand finale, Tone.

TONY. Showing them how to make a tent out of a sheet of brown paper went down well.

JOHN. Do you think so?

TONY. Mm. Added a bit of extra crackle to the crackling of the campfire John.

JOHN. Thanks Tone. I thought the best bit of the evening was when they asked their scoutmaster to do a turn and he did one about tent tidying.

TONY. What was it he said about tent pockets?

JOHN. If you have pockets in your tent you should tidy them but you don't need to bother with tidying the pockets in your trousers.

TONY. That's the one.

JOHN. Here's another biro, Tone. How was your sleep?

TONY. I dreamt about Dibby and Dobby.

JOHN. Oh them.

TONY. They were getting in a space ship and they were trying to give the driver Roman money.

JOHN. What a downer. It was great last night though.

TONY. It was a crackler, John.

JOHN. It was a crickle-crackler, Tony.

TONY. Do you think they enjoyed the pass-the-parcel?

JOHN. I think they'd have preferred the prize to have been a real frisbee.

TONY. They're glad we're letting them have the chair of leisure though.

JOHN. They are Tone, very glad. What did you think of that dance their scoutmaster did?

TONY. I don't think he needed to be naked.

JOHN. He wasn't!

TONY. He *was* in my dream, John.

I'm sorry about all that Skip stuff John. When you went to get the bike wheels I think I flipped a bit; I started remembering all this stuff with my father and I think his authoritarian streak just started coming out in me, it's weird, do you think it could happen again?

JOHN. Is that all the biros Tone?

TONY. Yeah.

JOHN. Rightyho let's go and get the dog.

JOHN. Well, Major, we're all packed up.

TONY. And we're ready for the off.

JOHN. Where's your other half?

MAJOR ROBBINGS. You mean Major Robbings's wife?

JOHN. No, I mean your shadow, where is it?

MAJOR ROBBINGS. It's in the shed.

MAJOR ROBBINGS'S WIFE. Hello lads, ready for the off are you?

TONY. Ah Major Robbings's wife, good morning, we're all ready for the off.

MAJOR ROBBINGS. Please don't swing on the gate.

JOHN. Why not? You sold off our property just for a few quid that you didn't even need. You betrayed our trust and ...

MAJOR ROBBINGS'S WIFE. You're not still going on about that are you?

MAJOR ROBBINGS. Forget all that. Come on in for a bowl of water.

JOHN. We've just come for the dog.

MAJOR ROBBINGS. Sheddie? I've put him out in the shed. He's in among the pile of hessian sacks we use for our potatoes.

JOHN. He was called Hermann when I left him.

MAJOR ROBBINGS'S WIFE. YOU give him a name and that's it, is it? No one else can give the dog a name that they think's more suitable?

MAJOR ROBBINGS. Relax, darling, relax. Look I'm sorry about the bicycle wheels you boys, no excuse for it, I admit I was wrong – and I'm sorry.

TONY. Well at least that's something John.

MAJOR ROBBINGS. And before you go I'd just like to

throw your sleeping bags into the river.

JOHN. What?

MAJOR ROBBINGS'S WIFE. He doesn't mean with you in them, stupid!

TONY. We've no time I'm afraid, we're ready for the off. Why would you want to do that though Major, just out of interest?

MAJOR ROBBINGS. To give you something to take away with you.

JOHN. Dirty river water?!

MAJOR ROBBINGS. Ah, you've changed your minds about the bowls of water, have you lads? Jolly good. Would you go and get the dog for them and bring my shadow while you're there, darling?

JOHN. I'll come and give you a hand with the dog.

TONY. It's not dirty river water we're having to drink, is it?

MAJOR ROBBINGS. No, just slightly murky.

TONY Why did you put the dog in the shed? It's not bonfire night.

MAJOR ROBBINGS. I like to think of the whole of life as a firework display.

TONY. You remind me of my mother.

MAJOR ROBBINGS. Why's that?

TONY. Crazy about potatoes.

MAJOR ROBBINGS. I don't particularly like potatoes.

TONY. No, but you're crazy, though, aren't you?

MAJOR ROBBINGS. Yes, I suppose I'm not, ha ha.

TONY. Ha ha.

In the shed

HERMANN. Look at that rake – it's as thin as a rake.

JOHN. How are you Hermann?

MAJOR ROBBINGS'S WIFE. Yes, Sheddie, how are you?

HERMANN. Listen you two, do you want to know what my name really is?

JOHN. No.

HERMANN. Typical.

JOHN. Useless name. Now listen Major Robbings's wife. Have you thought about whether you're willing to give it a go with me?

MAJOR ROBBINGS'S WIFE. I thought you understood: I stupidly projected a fantasy image and fortunately had the sense to see the truth of what you were without getting involved.

JOHN. That's a no, isn't it? Oh well, at least I've still got my pride.

MAJOR ROBBINGS'S WIFE. And your dog.

HERMANN. 'Ere, I'm not his dog. I'm mine.

On the way home

JOHN *and* TONY.
> We've heard the campfire crackle
> we've smelt the campfire smell
> we've been inside the countryside
> and inside our selves as well.

JOHN.
> We've been camping. Why?

TONY.
> Because we love it.

JOHN.
>We've been camping. Why?

TONY.
>Because it's great.

JOHN *and* TONY.
>We're cycling along
>cycling along
>singing our we're going home
>from going camping cycling song.

Back in the caff

JOHN. Harry, a couple of weak teas when you're ready. And would you be kind enough to put them in these camping mugs, we want to come back to non-camping reality in stages. Thanks a bundle. So what did you mean, Tone, when you said you'd remembered some stuff about your dad and it made you go all weird?

TONY. I meant my brother actually.

JOHN. Why did you say your dad?

TONY. Because I'd gone a bit weird.

JOHN. I thought you'd grown out of your weirdness by then?

TONY. So did I.

JOHN. What did you mean about your brother, then?

TONY. Talking about him putting his socks under my pillow brought back all his other bullying and made me want to assert myself and I went all weird.

JOHN. But you'd gone weird already at that point.

TONY. Had I? Weird. Thanks, Harry.

JOHN. Yeah. Cheers, Harry. Anyway let's drink our drink to another adventure.

TONY. Sorry?

JOHN. A toast, Tony.

TONY. I thought I'd made it clear that I wanted to be known as either Skip or Skipper? Do you want to remain a patrol leader or would you rather dig Harry here some latrines for his customers?

JOHN. Sorry about that, Skips.

TONY. No problem, John. Troop, troop alert!

___ Something missing upstairs _____

This man walks into an optician's and says 'excuse me
I'd like a replacement side piece for these glasses I'm
wearing.' 'But Sir, you're not wearing any glasses,' says
the optician. 'I'm sorry,' says the man, 'but for a minute
there I thought I was somebody else.'

___ Eating Bleary _____

Marooned,
they soon decided
that the necessary sacrifice
should be the one who'd lost his glasses,
the one they called Bleary.
They spooned him into their hunger
and the ordinariness of the meal
was eerie.

From the stable home

i

The Lord began
in inadequate accommodation:
straw instead of carpets
cows instead of dogs
and when he was a man
we aren't told
that he used his gold
to get hold
of somewhere decent.
I'd imagine he was saving himself
for his father's place.

ii *A chrimerick*

He started his life as a lad
in the worst room the innkeeper had
but the Lord was OK
'cos he knew that one day
he'd be in the big house with his dad.

This was my father

I knew him
like I knew the front of his hand.
I didn't understand his need to wallop me so
   much,
except that it kept us in touch.
Apart from skin and bone
I never knew
what he was made of
or afraid of,
in spite of all our time together
he was one of the strangers he warned me about
but without the sweets.

Popping into the optician's

One day John popped into the optician's and the
optician said 'good afternoon Sir, how can I help you?'
And John replied 'what I need is a new pair of glasses
that will indicate what people are up to behind my
back. It's my sister's husband I'm talking about and I
don't trust her brother either. He's a sly fox that one.'
'Certainly Sir,' said the optician. 'And will you be
wanting a tint with those?'

The gaps in the furniture get her down

There was an old woman from Goole
who had a laboratory stool
and she just couldn't stand
the hole for your hand
or the bits they'd cut out of her pool table.
Other things she was unable to get on with
were the coils of nothingness in amongst the bed springs
which reminded her of the nothingness between
  breakfast and lunch
and the emptiness in some of her drawers got her
  annoyed
as it caused her to reflect upon her hunch
that ultimately the void was all there is.
However all this was to change dramatically
the day she bumped into John as he burst angrily out
  of the optician's.

Judith

So you're not a myth.
You're the apple of my eye
and the orange of my glasses,
you're the succulence and pith.
Judith,
be my kin,
give us a kith.

Roger

Roger's in love with the teacher
but his love doesn't register.

Please Miss, Roger's having trouble
Roger's love is true
it says so on the inside of his desk
is there anything that you can do
to rescue Roger, Miss?

He's hoping for a sign
that says 'Roger, will you please be mine',
don't you realise why he keeps on coming up
   and sharpening his pencils?
I've seen him breaking them on purpose.

He's in short trousers now
but they'll soon be longer,
don't worry about his age Miss
who's to say that just because a person's older
their love is stronger?

When you put 'please see me'
it always pleases Roger
but he'd prefer it
if you could say 'please see me after school',
maybe down the outdoor swimming pool, Miss
the other kids don't go there in January.

Miss, Roger loves you.
But not as much as I do.

Without drought

The sky is spitting a lot
even though it is not
a footballer.

Where's the Comedy Tent?

The rain in Reading
was rodding up a flood
and there was mud
and sudden skidding.
'The Comedy Tent?'
the steward went.
'It's over there.
What's left of it.'
He indicated a large skeleton
bereft of canvas
and I asked if he was kidding.
It had gone up like a kite.

The previous night
the windy might
and the downpour's weight
were proof too great,
the roof had ripped
and the spreading had flown
as the Comedy Tent
did a turn of its own.

Glastonbury Festival field life

First night under canvas
two hours after the music finishes
the day begins,
with the sleep-shattering
aluminium clatter
of potential accommodation
tipped beside your ear,
accompanied by the natter
of those who have put away far too much 'gear'
to seriously consider these outsized spillikins.
They will have a go though
for the next two hours or so,
not knowing the difference
between a tent pole,
a toilet roll
and the megaphone they have brought along
to heckle the comedians.

The winner

In the Northern factory
it hadn't been easy
to gain acceptance,
being a student and a Southerner,
but one lunchtime
in the canteen
when one of the workers
observed that you could use
tomato ketchup to clean up old coins,
I said that it was better on your food
and the other lads congratulated me
on this piece of comedy
and I felt a stirring in my loins:
for the first time I had flirted with popular
    entertainment.

Spring rain

The April downpour brings
out three things:
the umbrella seller
the fragrance of pavements
and a lot of moisture.

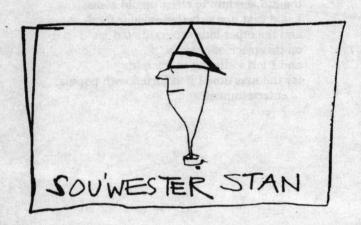

SOU'WESTER STAN

Bus conduct

After an undignified boarding,
with his can of Special Strength,
the old inebriate staggered half the length
of the crowded lower deck,
then levelled a dishevelled request
at a tidier young woman
to provide him with her seat.
Uncomplainingly she complied,
the sign said to give it up to the elderly
and social disadvantages aside
this man qualified
and after a slightly unsettling period of settling in
he was able to get on
with the business of belligerence
to persons unspecified
in relative comfort.

Wrong

I bought a one-day travel pass
and I lost it.
I got on a bus in a zone where the pass
would have been valid.
The conductor came by and didn't ask for my fare
and I thought is it wrong of me not to volunteer?
Technically I am fare-dodging.
But not in the eyes of God.

No more bus company

At the age of twenty-three
my mother sat me on her knee
and she said these words to me
she said 'Johnny,'
she said 'Johnny Boy.'
Now it may not sound like much to you
but it did the job I'm telling you
and I was gone out of the door
to get myself a job down at the depot,
down in Bristol,
City and Rovers town.
There were two machines and two of us
working the omnibus,
me I was the one behind
winding the handle up and bell-ringing
and on a good day singing as well:
'hello fellow travellers
it's good to have you on
you're all very beautiful
and you can call me Johnny Boy,
hold tight, all got tickets?
Hold tight, will you move on down.'
But I'll never get my job back now
not now those Bristol buses have gone OPO.
That's One Person Operation, gives a good
    conducting boy no hope-oh.
So who's going to help you get off and on?
Who's going to hand out the conversation?
Who's going to stand in the cubby hole,

who is going to say
'hold tight, all got tickets?
Hold tight, are you all right?
Hold tight, can I help you with that pushchair?
Hold tight, can I help you with that buggy
eyed baby?
Hold on very tightly.'

From another age

What looked like a broken window
in the phone box door
was actually a very small, lone,
levitating dinosaur.

Dark

There once was a doggie called Dark,
it was just the shadow of a dog,
a dog with no stuff,
so it was difficult to locate
when there wasn't any light in the lateness
but it was a good sort of dog to have
if you didn't have any garden.

The Lord's dog

She could jump as high as heaven.
She was the sheepdog the shepherds gave him
to help him save his flock,
the one he kept alive for thirty-three years
on one tin of God food.
You hear about the preaching and praying
but not about the Lord saying
'good dog, there's a good dog.'
Nor about all the tricks he taught her:
'walkies, walkies on the water.'
Nor about the way she barked at Pontius Pilate
and marked her master's loss
by marking out her territory
up against the cross
apostle.

A trip to the theatre

As I rambled over the ruined stage
of the Roman arena,
imagining the sword-bearing audience
of another age,
someone whose clothes looked cleaner
than mine, who must have seen a
sign that I had not
got somewhat
unreasonable:
'could you keep to the paths please,
you're setting a bad example to my son!'
Politely I explained the innocence of my
    misdemeanour
but inside,
my slighted pride
imagined how I might have been obscener,
or better still obscurer:
'Madam, under this world's wondrous dome
I walk where I want to
for I am a citizen of ancient Rome!'

Birthday in a Roman garden

At their meeting
she gives him a greeting
and a brooch wrapped in a colourful papyrus.
It is easily opened;
it has not been sealed with Sellotape.
He attaches the gift to his garment,
lifts his head
and feels the sea of inner sickness
as he sees on her person
the small red flower of another's passion.
'Where did you get it?' he blurts
and he hurts.
'The market in Ostia,' she replies.
'I mean the love-bite not the present,
whose is it?'
'It is mine,' she answers.
And for her intelligence he is thankful
and for her infidelity he is not.
He returns the brooch
and turns in his toga towards the sun
ignoring all of her imploring him to stay,
of which there is none.

Who am I?

A wider than average trousered cider drinker
with a spider
inside a box
and an unusual dog in her pocket.

Coming for Christmas

One year when I was at college
I rang my mum
and said that I needed to give the festive season a rest
because I was so behind in my work.
It was a lie,
I just wanted to give the festive season a rest.
I heard her call out to my dad
'he's not coming home for Christmas Bob.
It's the only time the family has together,' she chastised
    me.
'I'm sorry Mum, but this work is really important,'
    I defended.
'But you're only ever here for a couple of days.'
'I'm sorry Mum, I'll come home at Easter.'
'He said he won't be able to come home until
    Easter ...
you've made him cry now,
he's sitting here on the step and he's crying.
I've never made him cry,
you come home for Christmas and don't upset your
    father.'
'But he used to make me cry all the time when I was a
    boy.'
'Did he?'
'You know he did Mum.'
'All the more reason for you to come home then,'
she said, trying a more absurdist ploy.

The brief reunion
(La réunion brève)

In spite of all the beatings
and the bile
the thing I most remember about my father
is the smile he wore
the time he saw
his Parisian mother for the first time
in seventeen years
and I heard him talk his first language
for the first time in my life
and the tears flowed down their faces
as they nattered on like nut-cases.
She was a poor and very ancient woman
but somehow she'd got the money together
to come over and see her similarly unwealthy son.

The following morning after my dad had gone to work
my grandmother interrupted my mother's household
   duties
with the suggestion of an unscheduled coffee break.
When my dad came back that evening
and enquired as to the whereabouts of our visitor
my mum explained that she had had to go home early
because she was an old cow.

The return match

In my early teens
I used to go off my rocker
for soccer;
my room was chocca
block with spin offs from the game.
I supported Luton Town,
their manager was Allan Brown
and I can still name
his fourth division cup-winning line-up
but I won't.
My first professional writing job
was for a readers section
in the *Football Monthly*
for which I received a few bob
to corroborate
my team's fame.
Then I moved away to Bristol
and distance triumphed.
I tried to become a Rovers fan
but it was all over.
By the time I became a man of sorts
the sports pages held no interest for me
and Luton's entrance into the top flight
flew past unnoticed.
Twenty-five years later, asked to write
something about the team of my youth
for a fashionable magazine
I decided to return to the ground
to see if I was still Luton passion-proof.
It was January, they were playing Derby,

I had comps for the Directors' box and I felt like
   Jimmy Tarby.
Derby were the favourites,
the match began slowly
and slowly turned into a contest
and a suitable test of my attachment.
I was absorbed but not partisan.
Gradually the stars of the home side shone
and just before the interval Luton found the net.
I was appreciative but no more.
I didn't get out of my seat,
my only emotion was sadness that the gladness was
   really gone
and with half a heart I had my complimentary half-
   time coffee.
And then – ten minutes or so from the end
Luton's number eight collects the ball on the half-way
   line.
I remember that this was the number my hero wore
in Division Four – Ian Buxton it was then.
I look at my team sheet. Scott Oakes it is now.
I look up to see him beat three blokes.
Incredible skill
indelible skill
I'm on my feet
he's past a couple more
and within shooting distance – just.
He can't possibly score,
a soaring shot
Great Scott

it's there
a small prayer's answer
the tears come, the years go
and I'm one of the whole
I'm part of the roar
once more.

—— The Weekender continued ——

Saturday evening was designated in our Weekender's programme as a games evening and Mr Desk, the hotel manager, came into the lounge with a pile of board games which he placed on the table saying, 'Help yourselves everybody, be my guests.'

Mrs Phelps and I opted for the draughts and we had thirty games in all, all of which I won, although in no way did this detract from my partner's enjoyment. 'It's not the winning that counts, it's the contact with the wood,' she said, keeling over onto the parquet flooring. After a reviving cup of tea I suggested that perhaps she might like to retire. 'Yes I think I would,' she answered, 'and perhaps you might like to join me in church tomorrow morning?'

'Which church would that be?'

'The Church of Christ the Martian.'

'I don't believe I'm familiar with that one?'

'I'm the only member.'

'But where's the actual church?'

'It's in my heart.'

'How will I accompany you?'

'I'll set up a couple of candles in my room if you like.'

'What kind of service will it be though?'

'Room service,' said Mrs Phelps, for the first time allowing her comedic facility into our acquaintance.

In the chapel of Room 107 the next morning Mrs Phelps explained her denomination's thoughts on the Son of God.

'Well, originally he came down from Mars as a dog. Mary didn't give birth to him though, she caught him as he fell out of the spaceship and then put him in the manger, the same as it says in the Bible. Then one of the wise men gave him a pair of glasses which made him human ...'

'It sounds rather far fetched to me.'

'Yes, but not as far fetched as it sounds to people who knock on your door wanting to talk about religion.'

After the room service we embarked upon a snowy woodland walk during which I collected some bits for my contribution to the Weekender Fancy Dress Finale which I'd seen advertised in the hotel foyer.

Back in the warmth of the lounge I began to sew my costume and Mrs Phelps got on with some needlework of her own as we conversed in that slightly detached way that you might do in a primary school art lesson.

'But don't you think mobile phones and computers are a sign of progress?'

'Well, in a way I do, but really I think it's progress in the wrong direction.'

'Do you really?'

'Mm. I mean, there's more human interaction in a game of hopscotch than in a computer game.'

'That's true, but there's more chalk isn't there?'

'Yes ... What do you mean?' I said, half coming out of my reverie.

'Chalk makes a mess of the pavement doesn't it?'

'Oh right, but not of society. I think mobile phones and computer games and all that stuff isolate people; they're not really progress at all, they increase the sense of self but not the sense of community.'

'What about the sense of humour?'

'I think you'd better leave the jokes to me, Mrs Phelps. What do you think of these sleeves made of leaves I've made?'

'Very nice, John.'

That evening when I knocked on her door to go down to the party, Mrs Phelps appeared with a smile and a slice of cucumber, which she described to me as Martian holy communion.

'I'm nearly ready; and I won't be needing these,' she said, taking off her spectacles and turning into a dog.

My own costume was what I described as a bloke-tree; it consisted of the leaves I'd sewn onto my shirt and plenty of brown paper wrapped tightly about my legs. Soon I was hopping happily down the Grand Hotel staircase preceded by the excited yaps and yelps of Mrs Phelps, although apparently the notice I'd seen in the foyer was out of date and there was no fancy dress party scheduled for that evening.

My father's glasses

These glasses were my father's,
he left me them to keep,
he was an optician's clerk,
he got them on the cheap.
These glasses were my father's,
he saw the world through these
and sometimes what I'm looking at,
it seems my father sees.
'These lenses don't feel right,' he says,
'nothing's very clear.'
'What do you expect?' I answer,
'you're not really here, Dad.'

Please be reasonable

She heaved her dry white wine over his head,
it wasn't very dry.
He asked her if she believed this to be helping
   matters
then went to get a cloth and said
'why can't we just discuss the subject?
They're all very well these emotional responses
but what about taking some responsibility?'
Still she was defiant.
She likened him to a social worker.
And he likened her to a client.

Imminent death poem

goodbye sunshine
goodbye moon
I believe in poetry
I believe in life
and I be leavin' soon

Goodbye song

It's nearly time to leave you
it's almost time to go,
if you've just come in
and you're wondering if the show
is only just beginning
I'm afraid the answer's no.